Grammar Activities That Really Grab 'Em!

Grades 3–5

SARAH GLASSCOCK

New York • Toronto • London • Auckland • Sydney
Mexico City • New Delhi • Hong Kong • Buenos Aires

Teaching *Resources*

Editor: Sarah Longhi

Copy editor: Jeannie Hutchins

Cover design: Maria Lilja

Interior design: Melinda Belter

ISBN-13: 978-0-545-11265-9

ISBN-10: 0-545-11265-6

1 2 3 4 5 6 7 8 9 10 40 16 15 14 13 12 11 10

Contents

Introduction

It can be hard to convince students that grammar is a living, breathing thing that reflects not only the history of our language but also how language and its rules change in our contemporary lives. For example, today we try to use language more precisely to reflect the changes in our society by replacing *policeman* or *fireman* with *police officer* or *firefighter*. (We're still grappling with the wordiness of pairing *everyone* with the possessive pronouns *his* and *her*.) Grammar is simply a set of rules that helps us write and speak clearly so that others can understand what we mean. The aim of this book is to present an overview of major topics that will give your students tools to become better writers and speakers.

How to Use This Book

The book contains a mini-lesson for ten important grammar topics:

- Nouns
- Pronouns
- Verbs
- Adjectives and Adverbs
- Prepositions
- Singular and Plural Nouns and Verbs
- Subjects and Predicates
- Phrases and Clauses
- Elaboration
- Sentences

Each mini-lesson contains the following elements to support your teaching:

✔ A **teaching page** that focuses on introducing and defining the topic, teaching it in conjunction with a model passage, and applying it. A quote related to the topic begins each lesson and can be used as a springboard for introducing, discussing, or applying the grammar topic.

✔ A short **model passage** that shows important aspects of the grammar topic in action. You may want to display the passage onscreen to introduce or review the featured grammar points. Students can also keep this page in their notebooks or writing portfolios to guide them in their own writing.

✔ Two **writing prompts** that encourage students to write and share their work. You can photocopy the prompts on card stock and then cut them apart for students, write the prompts on the board, or display them onscreen. *With the Rest of the Class* tips help students extend their thinking by sharing their work with their peers.

✔ Three **activities** for the whole class, small group, pairs, or individuals that give students hands-on practice with the grammar topic. These activities require minimal preparation and appeal to a variety of learning styles; for example, students may play games, chant, or write ads and plays. Use the discussion tip *With the Class* to invite students to discuss the topic further.

✔ A **reproducible activity sheet** that goes with the activity featured in the Apply section of each teaching page.

You'll find some overlapping of topics. It's impossible, for example, to talk about subjects and predicates without talking about nouns, pronouns, and verbs, and it's impossible to talk about sentences without talking about all the other grammar topics in the book.

Immerse your students in an overview of each grammar topic or dive more deeply into one aspect. I hope this book encourages your students to see the powerful effect that grammar has on our words—and the effect we all have on our language.

All About Nouns

✳ The adjective hasn't been built that can pull a weak or inaccurate noun out of a tight place.

—William Strunk, Jr. and E. B. White

> You could say that a sentence revolves around its nouns. They tell the who or the what of a sentence. This mini-lesson focuses on the following aspects of nouns:
>
> - **singular and plural nouns**
> - **common and proper nouns**
> - **possessive nouns**
> - **descriptive nouns**

Introduction

Begin the mini-lesson by writing a short definition and example of a noun on the board, for example, "A noun names a person, animal, place, thing, or idea: <u>Chester</u> is a <u>poodle</u>. He loves the <u>freedom</u> of chasing <u>butterflies</u> in the wheat <u>field</u> behind his <u>doghouse</u>."

Teach

Distribute copies of the model passage "The Bumblebird and the Hummingbee" on page 7 to students. Ask them to follow along as you read it aloud. Then use the teaching guide on page 6 to discuss how the writer used nouns in the passage.

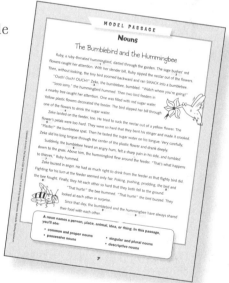

(Also see the lessons on pronouns, pages 11–16; singular and plural nouns and verbs, pages 35–40; and elaboration, pages 53–58.)

Apply

Hand out the Who Are You? reproducible on page 10. After going over the directions, model a few responses that describe yourself, for example, *person, teacher, hiker, cook, reader, deejay,* and so on. In your response, include nouns that will encourage students to realize how many different nouns they can use to describe themselves.

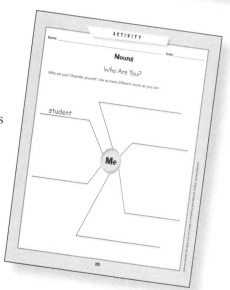

Singular and Plural Nouns

A singular noun refers to one person, place, animal, idea, or thing. A plural noun refers to more than one.

KEY POINTS

- Regular plural nouns are formed by adding –s or –es to the end of a singular noun.
- Irregular plural nouns such as *children, women, men, activities,* and *sheep* don't fit this pattern.
- Make a class list of the irregular plural nouns that students come across in their reading.

TEACHING WITH THE MODEL PASSAGE

4 A sentence can have a combination of singular and plural nouns in it. In this sentence, *bird, bill, one,* and *water* are singular. Only the noun *flowers* is plural.

7 *Thieves* is an irregular noun. The singular form of this noun is *thief*. Instead of adding –s to the end of *thief*, you change the final *f* to *v* and add –*es*.

Common and Proper Nouns

A common noun doesn't refer to a specific person, place, animal, thing, or idea. A proper noun does.

KEY POINTS

- A common noun is preceded by a definite or indefinite article—*the, a, an.*
- A proper noun is always capitalized.
- A common noun is only capitalized if it begins a sentence.

TEACHING WITH THE MODEL PASSAGE

3 The bumblebee's name is Zeke, which is a proper noun.

6 The writer used the common noun *bumblebee* here, but, for variety, she also could have used the proper noun *Zeke*.

8 These two common nouns are parallel. It would be strange to use one common noun and one proper noun in this sentence.

Possessive Nouns

A possessive noun tells who or what owns something.

KEY POINTS

- Possessive nouns indicate ownership; *the flower's petals* means the same as *the petals of the flower*.
- Singular possessive nouns are formed by adding 's to the end of the singular noun: *flower's*.
- Plural possessive nouns are formed by adding an apostrophe to the end of the plural noun: *flowers'*.

TEACHING WITH THE MODEL PASSAGE

2 To make the plural noun, *bushes*, possessive, add an apostrophe: *bushes'*.

5 To make the singular noun, *flower*, possessive, add an apostrophe s: *flower's*.

Descriptive Nouns

animal dog → poodle → Chester: The more specific you are in describing someone or something, the more your reader will enjoy your words.

KEY POINTS

Ask students to think about a story that only uses *the bird* for the main character. To be more specific and descriptive, the writer could substitute the kind of bird it is—*hummingbird*—and give it a human name—*Ruby*. Then the writer could use three different nouns to describe the bird.

TEACHING WITH THE MODEL PASSAGE

1 Instead of writing *tiny bird, fast bird,* or just *bird*, the writer tells exactly what kind of bird it is.

9 The writer has made up two nouns—*bumblebird* and *hummingbee*—to describe what happened when the bird and bee fought.

Nouns

The Bumblebird and the Hummingbee

Ruby, a ruby-throated hummingbird, darted through the garden. The sage bushes' red
1   2
flowers caught her attention. With her slender bill, Ruby sipped the nectar out of the flowers.
Then, without looking, the tiny bird zoomed backward and ran SMACK into a bumblebee.

"Ouch! *Ouch!* OUCH!" Zeke, the bumblebee, bumbled. "Watch where you're going!"
3

"Sooo sorry," the hummingbird hummed. Then two bird feeders in
a nearby tree caught her attention. One was filled with red sugar water.
Yellow plastic flowers decorated the feeder. The bird slipped her bill through
one of the flowers to drink the sugar water.
4

Zeke landed on the feeder, too. He tried to suck the nectar out of a yellow flower. The
flower's petals were too hard. They were so hard that they bent his stinger and made it crooked.
5
"Plastic!" the bumblebee spat. Then he tasted the sugar water on his tongue. Very carefully,
Zeke slid his long tongue through the center of the plastic flower and drank deeply.

Suddenly, the bumblebee heard an angry hum, felt a sharp pain in his side, and tumbled
6
down to the grass. Above him, the hummingbird flew around the feeder. "That's what happens
to thieves," Ruby hummed.
7

Zeke buzzed in anger. He had as much right to drink from the feeder as that flighty bird did.
Fighting for his turn at the feeder seemed only fair. Poking, pushing, prodding, the bird and
8
the bee fought. Finally, they hit each other so hard that they both fell to the ground.
8

"That hurts!" the bee hummed. "That hurts!" the bird buzzed. They
looked at each other in surprise.

Since that day, the bumblebird and the hummingbee have always shared
9   9
their food with each other.

**A noun names a person, place, animal, idea, or thing. In this passage,
you'll see:**

- **common and proper nouns**
- **possessive nouns**
- **singular and plural nouns**
- **descriptive nouns**

Nouns

Teachers: Duplicate these prompts on sturdy paper and then cut them apart. You may also write the prompts on the board or display them onscreen.

Name _____ Date _____

One or More Than One?

Write! Think of something that you'd really, really, really, *really* love to have. Then answer this question: *Would you like to have just one of these things—or would you like more than one?*

When you've finished writing, read over your work. Did you use singular nouns in the right places? Did you use plural nouns in the right places? Do all your subjects and verbs agree?

Write your full response on a separate sheet of paper.

With the Rest of the Class: Talk about the different things that everyone wants. Decide how to sort them into groups. Who do you think is most likely to get his or her wish? Which wish is the most fantastic or fanciful?

Name _____ Date _____

Guess That Noun

Write! Choose a person, animal, place, idea, or thing to write about. In other words, pick a noun. Write a description of it—but don't use the noun in your writing. You can use synonyms for the noun or other parts of speech to describe it. Exchange your description with a partner. Are you able to guess which noun your partner is describing?

Write your full response on a separate sheet of paper.

With the Rest of the Class: Talk about how you used the clues in your partner's work to figure out what the noun is.

Grammar Activities That Really Grab 'Em! Grades 3–5 © 2010 by Sarah Glasscock, Scholastic Teaching Resources

Activities: Nouns

Noun-Toss Ball Game

Materials: tennis ball or other small ball

Supply the group with a common noun for each round of play. To begin a round, say a common noun, such as *building,* and toss the ball to a student in the group. That student thinks of a more specific noun, such as *house,* and tosses the ball to someone else in the group. Then the second student thinks of another noun that's even more specific—or a proper noun—and tosses the ball to someone else in the group. If that student can't think of a noun, another round of play begins. The student holding the ball thinks of a new common noun, such as *shoe,* and tosses the ball. Record the nouns and keep score: Teams earn 3 points for a proper noun, 2 points for a more specific noun, 1 point for a new common noun.

With the Class: Discuss which common nouns had the longest and shortest lists of specific nouns. Ask: *Did you learn any new descriptive nouns that you'd like to use in your own writing?*

A Singular and Plural Picture Book

Materials: drawing paper, colored markers or colored pencils, crayons, folder, hole punch

Assign one or more different letters of the alphabet to each student. Then have your class write an alphabet animal picture book for younger readers. Each student should think of an animal whose name begins with each assigned letter. Encourage them to think of unusual animals that younger readers might not know. Each page should also include the singular and plural forms of the noun that names the animal. Give students the model at right to format each page.

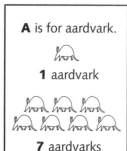

A is for aardvark.

1 aardvark

7 aardvarks

With the Class: Ask students to share their pages. Encourage older students to notice which of the plural nouns are regular and which are irregular. Compile the pages into a folder to create an alphabet book.

Does It Belong to Emma?

Pair students to play a possessive guessing game with the following directions:

1. Partner 1 looks around the classroom and secretly chooses an item that belongs to another student.

2. Partner 2 tries to guess who owns the item, writing each guess as a question: *Does it belong to Emma?*

3. Partner 1 writes the answers using possessive nouns: *It is not Emma's* or *It is Emma's.*

4. Once Partner 2 guesses the correct owner, Partner 1 can reveal what the item is.

5. Partners switch roles and play again.

With the Class: Discuss the following questions: Was it difficult to form a possessive noun out of anyone's name? Which letter does that name end with? Did you remember to add *'s* to the end of each name?

Name _____   Date _____

Nouns

Who Are You?

Who are you? Describe yourself. Use as many different nouns as you can.

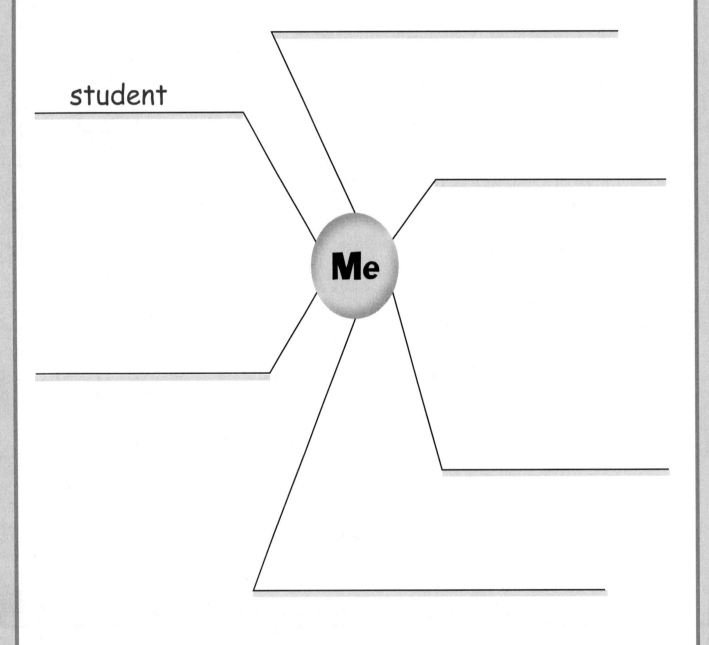

student

Me

Grammar Activities That Really Grab 'Em!, Grades 3–5 © 2010 by Sarah Glasscock, Scholastic Teaching Resources

All About Pronouns

 Good words by the third time will even bore the dogs.
—Chinese proverb

As the above proverb emphasizes, a reader will tire of even the most original noun if the writer repeats it too often. In addition to livening up sentences, pronouns add clarity and rhythm to them. This mini-lesson focuses on the following aspects of pronouns:

- **personal pronouns**
- **pronouns as subjects and objects**
- **pronoun agreement**
- **possessive pronouns**

Introduction

Begin a mini-lesson by writing a short definition of a pronoun on the board. Here's an example: "A pronoun takes the place of a noun in a sentence:

The dragon chased the girl, but she stopped it in its tracks with her slingshot."

Teach

Distribute copies of the model passage "All Fall Down!" on page 13 to students. Ask them to follow along as you read it aloud. Then use the teaching guide on page 12 to discuss how the writer used pronouns in the passage.

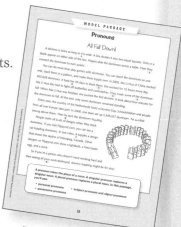

(Also see the lessons on prepositions, pages 29–34, and phrases and clauses, pages 47–52.)

Apply

Hand out the Who Says? reproducible on page 16 or display it onscreen. After reviewing the pronouns and usage examples, tell students that they can refer to the sheet as you play a game loosely based on Simon Says. Students respond with the appropriate action when they hear the words "[Pronoun] Says" but not when they hear "[Noun] Says." Continue until the class has correctly used all the personal subject pronouns several times.

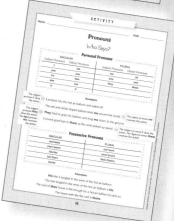

Example:

Teacher (point to self): Teacher says jump up and down. (Students do nothing.)

Teacher (points to Sarita, a student): She says . . . (Allow that student to supply the action.)

Sarita (points to herself): I say . . . whistle a tune. (Students whistle.)

Personal Pronouns
A personal pronoun takes the place of a noun in a sentence.

KEY POINTS
- A writer has to answer questions about number, gender, and the role of the noun in the sentence in deciding which pronoun to use to replace it.
- Remind students that a pronoun *replaces* a noun. In the following sentence, the pronoun *repeats* the subject instead of replacing it: <u>Jack</u>, <u>he</u> hopped over the candlestick.

TEACHING WITH THE MODEL PASSAGE
1 The pronoun *it* takes the place of the noun *domino* in this sentence. We use the pronoun *it* to talk about objects.

7 The writer doesn't know if the cat was a male or a female. She uses the pronoun *it* to replace *cat*.

Pronouns as Subjects and Objects
The subject pronouns are I, you, it, he, she, we, you, *and* they. *The object pronouns are* me, you, it, him, her, us, *and* them.

KEY POINTS
- Pronouns can replace subjects: <u>We</u> went outside. <u>She</u> slammed the door.
- Pronouns can replace nouns used as objects of prepositions or of verbs: The snow slid off the roof and fell <u>on us</u>. Mom told <u>us</u> to come inside.

TEACHING WITH THE MODEL PASSAGE
2 *They* takes the place of the noun *players*. Both the noun and pronoun are subjects. If the writer had replaced *dominoes* with *them* in this sentence, it would read: *They connect them to earn points.* That would be confusing because *they* and *them* replace two different nouns.

6 The writer knows that the acrobat was a man, so she used the subjective pronoun *he* to replace *acrobat*.

Pronoun Agreement
A singular pronoun takes the place of a singular noun. A plural pronoun takes the place of a plural noun.

KEY POINTS
- To avoid the *his-or-her* predicament, encourage students to rephrase singular subjects as plural subjects:

  A <u>student</u> should complete <u>his or her</u> homework every night.

  <u>Students</u> should complete <u>their</u> homework every night.

TEACHING WITH THE MODEL PASSAGE
3 The pronoun *her* is singular. It replaces the singular noun *Ma Li Hua*, which is a young woman's name. The plural pronoun *them* replaces the plural noun *dominoes*.

4 The pronoun *they* replaces the nouns *butterflies* and *cockroaches*. Both nouns are plural. If you wrote *a butterfly and a cockroach*, you would still use *they*. Both of these nouns are singular, but together, they make up a group. You replace the nouns with a plural pronoun.

Possessive Pronouns
A possessive pronoun shows ownership.

KEY POINTS
- The possessive pronouns are *my/mine, your/yours, its/its, our/ours, your/yours, their/theirs.*
- Possessive pronouns take the place of nouns, too. We can write or say *her slingshot* or *the slingshot is hers* instead of *the girl's slingshot*.
- Students may confuse the possessive pronouns *its* and *your* with the contractions *it's* and *you're*. Emphasize that a possessive pronoun never, ever contains an apostrophe.

TEACHING WITH THE MODEL PASSAGE
5 The dominoes belong to Ma Li Hua. She is a woman, so the writer uses the possessive pronoun *her* to show who the dominoes belong to.

8 Notice the homophones *your* and *you're*. They sound the same but have different meanings and spellings. *Your* is a possessive pronoun. *You're* is a contraction for the pronoun *you* and the verb *are*.

Pronouns

All Fall Down!

A domino is twice as long as it is wide. A line divides it into two equal squares. Dots or a
blank appear on either side of the line. Players slide the dominoes across a table. Then they
connect the dominoes to earn points.

You can do more than play games with dominoes. You can stand the dominoes on one
end, stack them in a pattern, and make them topple over. In 2003, Ma Li Hua of China stacked
303,628 dominoes. It took her 45 days to stack them. She worked for 10 hours every day.
Ma Li Hua also had to fight off butterflies and cockroaches. They made some of her dominoes
fall. When Ma Li Hua was finished, she pushed the first domino. It took about four minutes for
the dominoes to fall. At the end, only seven dominoes remained standing.

Every year, the country of the Netherlands hosts a Domino Day. Schoolchildren and people
from all over Europe take part. In 2008, one team set up 4,345,027 dominoes. An acrobat
swung above them. Then he sent the dominoes toppling.

People make all kinds of designs when they stack
dominoes. If you visit Flippycat.com, you can see a
cat toppling dominoes. In one video, it topples a design
that shows the skyline of Winnipeg, Canada. Other
designs on Flippycat.com show a lightbulb, a fried Easter
egg, and a clock.

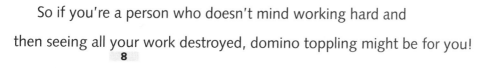

So if you're a person who doesn't mind working hard and
then seeing all your work destroyed, domino toppling might be for you!

**A pronoun takes the place of a noun. A singular pronoun replaces a
singular noun. A plural pronoun replaces a plural noun. In this passage,
you'll see:**

- **personal pronouns**
- **possessive pronouns**
- **subject pronouns and object pronouns**

Pronouns

Teachers: Duplicate these prompts on sturdy paper and then cut them apart. You may also write the prompts on the board or display them onscreen.

Name _____ Date _____

First, Second, or Third?

Write! Think about one of the funniest things that's ever happened to you. Write about what happened. Before you begin to write, decide whether to tell the story using one of the following points of view and its pronouns:

First person: *I, me, mine, my*

Second person: *you, yours, your*

Third person: *he, she, it, him, her, its, his, hers, its*

With the Rest of the Class: Explain how you decided which point of view and which pronouns to use to tell your story.

> Write your full response on a separate sheet of paper.

Name _____ Date _____

How Should I Phrase This?

Write! A prepositional phrase begins with a preposition and ends with a noun or a pronoun. Only objective pronouns—*me, you, it, her, him, us, them*—appear in prepositional phrases. Make a greeting card for friends or family members. Use one of the prepositional phrases below in your card. Complete the prepositional phrase with pronouns.

between _____ and _____

to _____ and _____

for _____ and _____

> Write your full response on a separate sheet of paper.

With the Rest of the Class: Display your cards. Compare the different ways everyone completed the prepositional phrases and used them in the cards.

Grammar Activities That Really Grab 'Em!, Grades 3–5 © 2010 by Sarah Glasscock, Scholastic Teaching Resources

Activities: Pronouns

The No-Pronouns Writing Zone

Materials: classroom object, timer

PAIR Set the timer for one minute. Tell students to use the time to examine an object. When the time is up, have them write three to five sentences to describe it—without using any pronouns!

After students have stopped writing, give them the following instructions: Exchange descriptions with your partner. Decide which nouns to replace with pronouns. Write the revised description on a new sheet of paper. Then hold a conference with your partner. Explain how you decided which nouns to replace. Listen as your partner talks about adding pronouns to your description. Do you agree with the changes? If not, rewrite your description—but don't forget the pronouns.

With the Class: Talk about how it felt to use only nouns in your description. Ask: *Was it harder or easier than you thought it would be?* Then have students share their thoughts about adding the pronouns.

Add It Up

Materials: pair of number cubes, paper and pencils

PAIR **WHITE BOARD** Have students take turns rolling a number cube to generate numbers for an addition or subtraction sentence. For example, if the first student rolled a 5 and the second student rolled a 4, they could write either of these sentences: 5 – 4 = 1 or 5 + 4 = 9. (Have them roll two number cubes to produce double-digit numbers.) Tell pairs to write a word problem to go with their addition or subtraction sentence and to include both nouns and pronouns in their word problem.

With the Class: Encourage pairs to share their word problems with classmates. Guide a discussion about how students worked together to create their word problems.

Yours, Mine, and Ours

SMALL GROUP Ask the group to identify some of their favorite movie or book titles. You might volunteer some pronoun-heavy titles, such as *Them!*, a movie about giant ants, or *Yours, Mine, and Ours,* a movie about a blended family. Then challenge groups to create their own movie and book titles that contain pronouns and no nouns and then to write a brief summary of each movie and book. Give the following hints:

- To get started, groups can work with existing titles and replace the nouns with the appropriate pronouns.

- Two nouns, such as *Lola and Martin,* can be replaced with *She and he* or *They.*

With the Class: Ask groups to share their titles with the rest of the class. Discuss which titles did the best job of describing the movie or book.

Name _____ Date _____

Pronouns

Who Says?

Personal Pronouns

SINGULAR		PLURAL	
Subject Pronouns	*Object Pronouns*	*Subject Pronouns*	*Object Pronouns*
I	me	we	us
you	you	you	you
he	him	they	them
she	her		
it	it		

Examples

The subject pronoun **I** does the action.

I jumped into the hot air balloon and sailed off.

The red-and-white striped balloon took **me** around the world.

The object pronoun **me** receives the action.

The subject pronoun **they** does the action. The object pronoun **me** receives the action.

They tried to grab the balloon and drag **me** down to the ground.

I waved good-bye to **them** as the wind picked up speed.

The subject pronoun **I** does the action. The object pronoun **them** receives the action.

Possessive Pronouns

SINGULAR	PLURAL
my/mine	our/ours
your/yours	your/yours
his/his	their/theirs
her/hers	
its/its	

Examples

His kite is tangled in the wires of the hot air balloon.

The kite tangled in the wires of the hot air balloon is **his**.

The roof of **their** house is flat enough for a hot air balloon to land on.

The house with the flat roof is **theirs**.

Grammar Activities That Really Grab 'Em!, Grades 3–5 © 2010 by Sarah Glasscock, Scholastic Teaching Resources

All About Verbs

 Life is a verb. Life is living, living is doing.

—Charlotte Perkins Gilman

> Verbs are the energy sources of sentences. They set their subjects into motion—whether a subject is walking or simply being. This mini-lesson focuses on the following aspects of verbs:
>
> - **verb tenses**
> - **irregular verbs**
> - **subject-verb agreement**
> - **descriptive verbs**

Introduction

Begin a mini-lesson by writing a short definition of verbs on the board, for example: "A verb shows action: The dog <u>howls</u>. A verb also can show a state of being: The dog <u>is</u> wet."

Teach

Distribute copies of the model passage "Towers Stretching to the Sky" on page 19 to students. Ask them to follow along as you read it aloud. Then use the teaching guide on page 18 to discuss how the writer used verbs in the passage.

(Also see the lessons on singular and plural nouns and verbs on pages 35–40 and subjects and predicates on pages 41–46.)

Apply

Hand out the Create a New Word reproducible on page 22 and go over the information about sniglets. You may want to mention that an executive chair is a chair that has arms and moves on wheels. Ask students: *Do you see how the words* executive *(a noun) and* glide *(a verb) were blended to create the new verb?* Before students work on their own sniglets, remind them to follow the same format as the entry for *execuglide.*

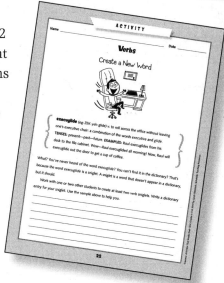

Verb Tenses
Verb tenses show time. Action can occur in the past, present, or future.

KEY POINTS
- Point out that although most of the verbs in this personal narrative are in the past tense, students will also spot verbs in the present and future tenses.

- Encourage students to look for key words and phrases that help signal which tense to use.

TEACHING WITH THE MODEL PASSAGE

1 *Constructed* is a past-tense verb. The words *last summer* show that the action occurred in the past.

8 *I'm thinking* means *I am thinking. Am thinking* is in the present tense. The word *now* shows that the action is occurring in the present.

9 *Will construct* is a future-tense verb. The words *next summer* show that the action will take place in the future.

Irregular Verbs
Regular past tense verbs are formed by adding –ed to the present tense of the verb. Irregular verbs don't follow this rule.

KEY POINTS
- Review the differences between regular and irregular verb forms. Share the fact that many of the irregular verbs in English are very old words that are still formed using old rules. For instance, the verb *drink* comes from the Old English word *drincan*. Its past tense was *dranc.*

TEACHING WITH THE MODEL PASSAGE

5 *Came* is the past tense of *come.* It's an irregular verb.

6 The present tense of *dug* is *dig,* which is an irregular verb.

Subject-Verb Agreement
Subjects and verbs must agree. A singular subject always takes a singular verb. A plural subject always takes a plural verb.

KEY POINTS
- Remind students that a complete sentence needs both a subject and a verb. The subject and verb may be singular or plural, but they must always agree with each other.

TEACHING WITH THE MODEL PASSAGE

2 *We* is a plural noun. It takes a plural verb: *were working.*

4 Sometimes the subject and verb are separated by a prepositional phrase. The simple subject is *none,* not *towers. None* is singular, so it takes the singular verb *was destroyed.*

Descriptive Verbs:
Verbs with a lot of muscle make writing more descriptive.

KEY POINTS
- Emphasize how using different synonyms for a common action verb such as *move* (e.g., *walk, dance, shuffle*) can make our speech or writing more accurate and interesting. Have volunteers demonstrate the three actions to highlight the differences among the verbs.

- Remind students to think about using strong verbs that create vivid pictures in a reader's mind.

TEACHING WITH THE MODEL PASSAGE

3 The verbs *blasted* and *flooded* show the action—and the power—of the water.

7 Water doesn't have arms and legs. It can't really crawl, but the verb *crawled* shows that the water moved slowly but surely up the beach toward the castle.

9 Think about using synonyms: *construct* is a good replacement for *build* or *make.*

Verbs

Towers Stretching to the Sky

Last summer, my cousins and I constructed an enormous sand castle on the beach in Port
1
Aransas, Texas. We didn't progress very far on our first castle. We were working too close to the
2
water. The waves blasted the tower and flooded the rest of the castle. Then we got smart and
3   **3**
moved our construction site five feet from the water.

Soon four tan sand towers stretched up toward the sky. None of the towers was destroyed
4
by the waves. They all stood tall. We even made flags and stuck one on each tower. People
came from all over the beach to watch us work. A lot of them had ideas about what we should
5
add to our castle, but we had our own ideas.

The last thing we constructed was a moat. We dug a ditch around our castle. When the tide
6
slowly crawled up the beach, the water gently filled the moat. Our parents snapped a photo of
7
us standing in back of our castle. We almost disappeared behind the tall towers.

I'm thinking about how to make an even larger sand castle next summer and drawing up
8
plans now. Next summer, maybe we will construct a full-size castle in the sand!
9

A verb describes an action or a state of being. In this passage,
you'll see:

- **verb tenses**
- **subject-verb agreement**

- **irregular verbs**
- **descriptive verbs**

Grammar Activities That Really Grab 'Em!, Grades 3–5 © 2010 by Sarah Glasscock, Scholastic Teaching Resources

Verbs

Teachers: Duplicate these prompts on sturdy paper and then cut them apart. You may also write the prompts on the board or display them onscreen.

- -

Name _____ **Date** _____

Yesterday, Today, Tomorrow

Write! Choose one of the prompts below to write about. Pay attention to the verb tense!

- Think back to when you were in the first grade. What is the most important event you remember? Use only the past tense to describe what happened.

- What is the most interesting thing you're learning right now in school? Why is it so interesting to you? Use only the present tense in your response.

- What do you think being grown-up will be like? What will you do for a living? Where will you live? Use only the future tense to predict what will happen.

Write your full response on a separate sheet of paper.

With the Class: Talk about why you chose the past, the present, or the future. Was writing in that tense easier or more difficult than you thought it might be?

- -

Name _____ **Date** _____

The Tyrannosaurus Rex Growled . . .

Write! What if you could step into a time machine? What place would you visit? Would you travel to the past or to the future? What would you experience? What would you see, hear, smell, taste, and feel? What would you do? Write a story about your adventures. Use the present tense, even if you visit the past or the future.

Exchange stories with a partner. Read the story and then think about how the writer used verbs. Did the choice of verbs really help you "see" the story? Talk about what you liked about the story and ask any questions you have.

Write your full response on a separate sheet of paper.

With the Rest of the Class: Read your story aloud to the class. Share how your partner helped you revise your work.

Grammar Activities That Really Grab 'Em!, Grades 3–5 © 2010 by Sarah Glasscock, Scholastic Teaching Resources

Activities: Verbs

That's Highly Irregular

Materials: picture books, chapter books, or leveled readers; dictionary

 Remind students that we form the past tense of a regular verb by adding *–ed*: *jump + –ed = jumped*. Irregular verbs don't follow this rule: *eat → ate; bring → brought*. Challenge partners to see how many regular and irregular verbs they can find in a book of their choice. Have them open the book to any page and list at least 15 verbs. Tell partners to identify the tense and tell whether the verb is regular or irregular and create and complete a chart like this one:

Verb	Tense	Regular or Irregular?	How do you know?
see	present	irregular	Past tense is <u>saw</u>, not <u>see + –ed</u>.

If they have any questions about a verb, they should look it up in the dictionary.

With the Class: Discuss how students decided whether a verb was regular or irregular. Did any of the verbs fool them?

Do You Agree?

Materials: 52 index cards, four markers for each group

 Form groups of four players. Have each player write a set of 13 cards: One writes 13 different singular nouns; one writes 13 different plural nouns; one writes 13 different singular verbs; one writes 13 different plural verbs. Tell students that they're going to play a card game that's similar to Go Fish called Do You Agree? Give them these instructions:

1. Place all the cards facedown and mix them up. Each player draws 13 cards.

2. Take turns laying down a card from your hand and asking the other players for a card that agrees with it, for example: "Singular verb—give me a singular noun." If a player has the card you ask for, he or she gives it to you. Ask the other players, "Do you agree?" If they think that subject and verb agree, you keep the card. If a player doesn't have the card, the next player takes a turn.

3. Play continues clockwise until all the matches have been made.

With the Class: Talk about why nouns such as *family* and *group* take singular verbs.

Hello, Math Hotline—Tell Me What to Do!

 Announce that students have a new job on the Math Hotline. They must help their peers by writing the steps for solving a math problem. Choose a math topic that students need to review; it might be finding the sum of three numbers, writing a fraction, subtracting decimals, or identifying a rectangle. Show how to solve a sample problem by breaking down the solution into steps and writing clear directions that contain precise verbs.

With the Class: Have groups exchange work. Are they able to solve each other's problems using the directions? Collect directions in a Math Hotline notebook for everyone to refer to.

Name _____ Date _____

Verbs

Create a New Word

{ **execuglide** (eg-ZEK-yeh-glide) *v.* to roll across the office without leaving one's executive chair: a combination of the words *executive* and *glide*. **TENSES:** present—past—future. **EXAMPLES:** Raul execuglides from his desk to the file cabinet. Wow—Raul execuglided all morning! Now, Raul will execuglide out the door to get a cup of coffee. }

What? You've never heard of the word *execuglide*? You can't find it in the dictionary? That's because the word *execuglide* is a sniglet. A sniglet is a word that doesn't appear in a dictionary, but it should.

Work with one or two other students to create at least two verb sniglets. Write a dictionary entry for your sniglet. Use the sample above to help you.

_____

_____

_____

_____

_____

_____

Grammar Activities That Really Grab 'Em!, Grades 3–5 © 2010 by Sarah Glasscock, Scholastic Teaching Resources

All About Adjectives and Adverbs

✳ I do not like green eggs and ham. I do not like them, Sam-I-am.
—Dr. Seuss

✳ As to the Adjective; when in doubt, strike it out
—Mark Twain

> Adjectives modify nouns and pronouns. Adverbs modify verbs, adjectives, and other adverbs. This mini-lesson focuses on the following aspects of adjectives and adverbs:
>
> - **adjectives modifying nouns and pronouns**
> - **adverbs modifying verbs, adjectives, and other adverbs**
> - **positive, comparative, and superlative forms**
> - **descriptive adjectives and adverbs**

Introduction

After reviewing the definition of adjectives and adverbs, share Dr. Seuss's quote with students. Challenge them to replace the adjective *green* with as many adjectives and adverbs as they can. You may want to start with your own example, such as "I do not like moss green eggs and extremely tough ham." When Dr. Seuss's original sentence is overloaded with adjectives and adverbs, read aloud Mark Twain's quote. Work with students in deciding which adjectives—and adverbs—to strike out. Did students decide to scale back all the way and stick with "green eggs and ham"?

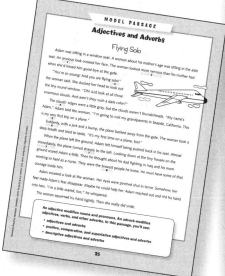

Teach

Distribute copies of the model passage "Flying Solo" on page 25 to students. Ask them to follow along as you read it aloud. Then use the teaching guide on page 24 to discuss how the writer used adjectives and adverbs in the passage.

Apply

Give each student a copy of the reproducible That's Quite a Character! on page 28. Have a variety of colored markers and colored pencils on hand. Go over the directions with students, and on a copy of the page, model drawing a visual detail on the character shape. Show them how you would write a description of that detail below the drawing. Display students' completed reproducibles and encourage everyone to talk about his or her work.

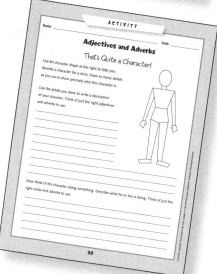

Adjectives
Adjectives modify nouns and pronouns.

KEY POINTS

- An adjective usually appears before the noun or pronoun it modifies, but it can follow verbs such as *be, feel, smell, sound, tastes, look, appear,* and *seem.*

- Encourage students to switch the order and location of the adjectives in the third sentence in the passage and talk about how the rearrangement changes the meaning and clarity.

TEACHING WITH THE MODEL PASSAGE

1 The adjectives *an* and *anxious* modify the noun *look.* Articles such as *a, an,* and *the* always go first in a series of adjectives.

4 The apostrophe in *clouds'* shows that this adjective is possessive. It modifies *edges.* You could also write, *the edges of the clouds.*

Adverbs
Adverbs modify adjectives, verbs, and other adverbs.

KEY POINTS

- An adverb can appear almost anywhere in a sentence. In general, it goes before a simple verb.

- It's okay to separate a verb with an adverb: *We will <u>probably</u> go to the baseball game.*

TEACHING WITH THE MODEL PASSAGE

5 The adverb *very* modifies the adjective *first. First* modifies the noun *trip.* You couldn't move *very* to another place in the sentence. It goes with the adjective, and the adjective can't be moved.

6 *Suddenly* is an adverb that modifies the verb *backed.* Try placing it after these words: *plane, away,* and *gate*—each new placement creates a different emphasis.

Positive, Comparative, and Superlative Forms
The positive form describes one thing. The comparative form compares two things. The superlative form compares more than two things.

KEY POINTS

- An adjective or adverb in a positive state describes one thing (*red, slowly*).

- The comparative is formed by adding *-er* to the end of positive adjectives or adverbs or by adding *more* or *less* in front of them (*redder, more slowly*).

- The superlative is formed by adding *-est* to the end of positive adjectives or adverbs or by adding *most* or *least* in front of them (*reddest, most slowly*).

TEACHING WITH THE MODEL PASSAGE

2 The comparative *more nervous* compares two people: the woman and Adam's mother. You can often figure out whether to add *-er* or *more* by trying to say both forms: *nervouser/more nervous.* Point out that some comparatives and superlatives are irregular: *good, better, best.*

8 Adam is comparing his father and mother to all the people he knows, so the writer uses the superlative form of the adjective: *brave + -est.*

Descriptive Adjectives and Adverbs
Descriptive adjectives and adverbs are as important to use in expository and persuasive writing as they are in narrative nonfiction and fiction.

KEY POINTS

- As students explore the power of adding adjectives and adverbs, their work may get a little florid. Better to let them stretch their vocabularies than to have them stick with the same adjectives and adverbs. However, do bring up the Mark Twain quote on page 23 when you think students need some constructive help in pruning their descriptions.

TEACHING WITH THE MODEL PASSAGE

3 The adverb *solo* modifies the verb *are flying.* The writer could have used the adverb *alone* instead, but *solo* reveals a little something about the woman and how she speaks.

7 The adverbs *immediately* and *sharply* describe when and how the plane turned. Adam's stomach probably dropped when the plane did this. Did students' stomachs drop, too?

Adjectives and Adverbs

Flying Solo

Adam was sitting in a window seat. A woman about his mother's age was sitting in the aisle
seat. An anxious look crossed her face. The woman looked more nervous than his mother had
    1   **2**
when she'd kissed him good-bye at the gate.

"You're so young! And you are flying solo!"
                                3
the woman said. She ducked her head to look out
the tiny round window. "Oh! Just look at all those
enormous clouds. And aren't they such a dark color?"

The clouds' edges were a little gray, but the clouds weren't thunderheads. "My name's
         4
Adam," Adam told the woman. "I'm going to visit my grandparents in Seaside, California. This
is my very first trip on a plane."
    5
Suddenly, with a jerk and a bump, the plane backed away from the gate. The woman took a
    6
deep breath and tried to smile. "It's my first time on a plane, too!"

When the plane left the ground, Adam felt himself being pushed back in his seat. Almost
immediately, the plane turned sharply to the left. Looking down at the tiny houses on the
   7   **7**
ground scared Adam a little. Then he thought about his dad fighting in Iraq and his mom
working so hard as a nurse. They were the bravest people he knew. He must have some of that
                                    8
courage inside him.

Adam sneaked a look at the woman. Her eyes were pinched shut in terror. Somehow, her
fear made Adam's fear disappear. Maybe he could help her. Adam reached out and slid his hand
into hers. "I'm a little scared, too," he whispered.

The woman squeezed his hand tightly. Then she really did smile.

> **An adjective modifies nouns and pronouns. An adverb modifies
> adjectives, verbs, and other adverbs. In this passage, you'll see:**
>
> - **adjectives and adverbs**
> - **positive, comparative, and superlative adjectives and adverbs**
> - **descriptive adjectives and adverbs**

Adjectives and Adverbs

Teachers: Duplicate these prompts on sturdy paper and then cut them apart. You may also write the prompts on the board or display them onscreen.

- -

Name _____ Date _____

More Than Bread and Cheese

Write! Daydream about a grilled cheese sandwich. What does it look like? How does it smell and taste? How does it feel in your mouth? What do you hear when you bite into the sandwich? Write a sentence—or a poem—describing a grilled cheese sandwich. Use all your senses and tasty adjectives to describe it. Try to make your readers wish they were eating that sandwich, too.

> Write your full response on a separate sheet of paper.

With the Rest of the Class: Read your description aloud to a small group. Talk about how the adjectives helped you imagine the sandwich. Does your description make everyone hungry?

- -

Name _____ Date _____

How Late or Early Were You?

Write! Think about a time when you arrived very late or very early somewhere. Why didn't you arrive on time? How did you feel? Write a short paragraph describing what happened. Tell *exactly* how late or early you were. Use adverbs in your description. Do not include overused adverbs such as *very, really, pretty, so.*

> Write your full response on a separate sheet of paper.

With the Rest of the Class: Share your writing with a partner. Look at the adverbs your partner used. Did you use any of those adverbs, too? Which adverbs surprised you most?

Grammar Activities That Really Grab 'Em!, Grades 3–5 © 2010 by Sarah Glasscock, Scholastic Teaching Resources

Activities: Adjectives and Adverbs

Absolutely, Positively Not

Materials: a dictionary for each team

 Tell students that, often, adding *–ly* to an adjective can turn it into an adverb.

Examples: *adjective:* rapid   *adverb:* rapidly   *adjective:* slow   *adverb:* slowly

Form two teams, the Adjectives and the Adverbs. The Adjectives think of 15 adjectives. Most of the adjectives should turn into adverbs when *–ly* is added to the end. However, not all the adjectives should fit that pattern, for example, colors such as *red* and *blue*. Then the Adjective team calls out an adjective. If they can, the Adverbs turn the adjective into an adverb by adding *–ly*. If they can't form an adverb, they say, "Absolutely, positively not." As referee, you'll have the final say, but allow teams to use the dictionary if there is a disagreement over the answer. Then students switch teams and play again.

With the Class: How are the meanings of the adjective *rapid* and the adverb *rapidly* connected? Are the adjective *hard* and the adverb *hardly* connected in the same way?

Fast, Faster, Fastest

Materials: 30 index cards, markers, dictionary

Make ten sets of adjective and adverb cards or have the groups do so. Each set should show the positive, comparative, and superlative forms of the adjective or adverb.

Examples: | fast | faster | fastest | | slippery | more slippery | most slippery |

Place the cards in three different stacks (1—positive form, 2—comparative form, 3—superlative form) and write the corresponding number on the blank side of each card. Remind students to keep each stack of cards in order and then have them exchange the three stacks of cards with another group.

Give the following directions for a card game: Place the three stacks of cards with the numbered sides up. Decide who will be players 1, 2, and 3. Player 1 turns over a card in the 1 pile. Players 2 and 3 have to supply the correct comparative and superlative forms of the adjective or adverb. You may look up the word in the dictionary. Then turn over cards 2 and 3 to see if you're correct. Then Player 2 turns faceup a card in the 2—comparative pile. Players 1 and 3 have to supply the correct positive and superlative forms. Player 3 goes next.

With the Class: Talk about the easiest and most difficult comparative and superlative forms of the adjectives and adverbs students formed. How often did they look in the dictionary?

And That's the Whole Story

To the Teacher: Compile all the stories in a binder or a folder.

 Who did students describe on the That's Quite a Character! reproducible? Tell them to write a story about that character. Remind students to use adjectives and adverbs to help them describe the character and the setting.

With the Class: Have students read all the stories. Then discuss what they noticed about how the other writers used adjectives and adverbs.

Name _____   Date _____

Adjectives and Adverbs

That's Quite a Character!

Use the character shape at the right to help you describe a character for a story. Draw as many details as you can to show precisely who this character is.

Use the details you drew to write a description of your character. Think of just the right adjectives and adverbs to use.

_____

_____

_____

_____

_____

_____

_____

_____

Now think of this character doing something. Describe what he or she is doing. Think of just the right verbs and adverbs to use.

_____

_____

_____

_____

_____

All About Prepositions

 This land was made for you and me.
—Woody Guthrie

A preposition shows the connection between a noun or a pronoun and the rest of a sentence. This mini-lesson focuses on the following aspects of prepositions:

- **purpose of prepositions**
- **prepositional phrases**

Introduction

Begin a mini-lesson by writing a short definition of prepositions on the board, for example: "A preposition connects a noun or a pronoun to the rest of the sentence: The kitten hid <u>under</u> the table."

Teach

Distribute copies of the passage "A Long Bicycle Ride Up and Down Mountains," on page 31 to students. Read it aloud and ask them to follow along. Then use the teaching guide on page 30 to discuss how the writer used prepositions in the passage.

(Also see the lessons on pronouns on pages 11–16 and phrases and clauses on pages 47–52.)

Apply

Duplicate the Jigsaw Puzzle reproducible on page 34 onto card stock; make a copy for each student. Go over the prepositions at the top of the page and then the directions for labeling the puzzle pieces. Model how you would label the first two puzzle pieces. Monitor students' progress and offer guidance as necessary—when they label their pieces and when they solve their partners' puzzles. Allow time for students to talk about how they used the preposition clues to put the pieces together.

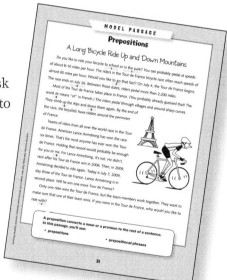

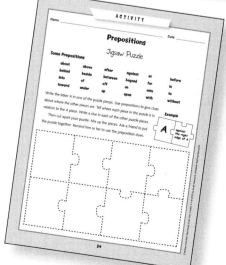

Prepositions

Prepositions connect nouns and objective pronouns to the rest of the sentence and give us information about their relationship to the sentence, including time, place, location, and movement.

KEY POINTS

- It's okay to end a sentence with a preposition—as long as the preposition can't be deleted from the sentence.

  Correct: *Who are you going with?*

  Incorrect: *Where do you live at?*

  If you're still in doubt, think about this quotation from Winston Churchill: "Ending a sentence with a preposition is something up with which I will not put."

TEACHING WITH THE MODEL PASSAGE

2 The word *to* is most often used as a preposition. In this sentence, however, it is part of the infinitive verb *to go*.

4 Many other languages, such as French and Spanish, have prepositions, too.

5 There are about 100 prepositions in the English language. Each has a different meaning. The prepositions in this sentence are *up* and *down*. Ask students to try using *under*, *through*, or *with* in the sentence instead. Does the sentence still make sense?

7 You can end a sentence with a preposition. Say the sentence without the preposition. If it doesn't make sense, keep the preposition at the end. If it does make sense, get rid of the preposition.

Prepositional Phrases

A prepositional phrase begins with a preposition and ends with an object pronoun.

KEY POINTS

- The pronoun in a prepositional phrase is always an object pronoun—*me, you, him, her, it, us, you, them.*

- A prepositional phrase that has two pronouns or a noun and pronoun tends to trip up people, and they use a subject pronoun instead of an object pronoun: *for you and I* (which is incorrect) instead of *for you and me.*

TEACHING WITH THE MODEL PASSAGE

1 This sentence has two prepositional phrases: *to school* and *in the park*. Ask: *What is the difference between riding* to *school and riding* in *the park? How does each preposition help you tell the difference?*

3 Some prepositional phrases can appear in different places in a sentence. You could move the prepositional phrase in this sentence: *On July 26, the race ends.*

6 Remind students that a pronoun in a prepositional phrase has to be objective. *Me* is an objective pronoun. Although students might write or say *for you and I*, they probably wouldn't write or say *for I*.

Prepositions

A Long Bicycle Ride Up and Down Mountains

Do you like to ride your bicycle to school or in the park? You can probably pedal at speeds
of about 8–10 miles per hour. The riders in the Tour de France bicycle race often reach speeds of
almost 60 miles per hour. Would you like to go that fast? On July 4, the Tour de France begins.
The race ends on July 26. Between those dates, riders pedal more than 2,200 miles.

Most of the Tour de France takes place in France. (You probably already guessed that! The
word *de* means "of" in French.) The riders pedal through villages and around sharp curves.
They climb up the Alps and down them again. By the end of

the race, the bicyclists have ridden around the perimeter
of France.

Teams of riders from all over the world race in the Tour
de France. American Lance Armstrong has won the race
six times. That's the most anyone has ever won the Tour
de France. Holding that record would probably be enough
for you or me. For Lance Armstrong, it's not. He didn't
race after his Tour de France win in 2006. Then, in 2009,
Armstrong decided to ride again. Today is July 7, 2009,
day three of the Tour de France. Lance Armstrong is in
second place. Will he win one more Tour de France?

Only one rider wins the Tour de France, but the team members work together. They want to
make sure that one of their team wins. If you were in the Tour de France, who would you like to
ride with?

**A preposition connects a noun or a pronoun to the rest of a sentence.
In this passage, you'll see:**

- **prepositions**
- **prepositional phrases**

Prepositions

Teachers: Duplicate these prompts on sturdy paper and then cut them apart. You may also write the prompts on the board or display them onscreen.

✂ -

Name _____ **Date** _____

This Land . . .

Write! Woody Guthrie was a singer and a songwriter. In 1940, he wrote a song about America called "This Land Is Your Land." Here are some lines of his song:

> *This land is your land, this land is my land*
>
> *From California, to the New York Island;*
>
> *From the redwood forest, to the Gulf Stream waters*
>
> *This land was made for you and me.*

Think about the last line of the song: "This land was made for you and me." What do these words mean to you?

Write your full response on a separate sheet of paper.

With the Rest of the Class: Identify the prepositional phrase in the last line of the song. What do you notice about it? Then talk about what words you could add to the song to tell about the place where you live.

✂ -

Name _____ **Date** _____

My Room

Write! Draw a picture of your room at home. Then choose one object in your drawing to write about. Imagine that the drawing and your words are one page in a picture book. Think about how to use prepositions and prepositional phrases in your description of the object. Which prepositions help show its location or its place in relationship to other parts of the room?

With the Rest of the Class: Share your work with the rest of the class. Talk about the different ways you and your classmates used prepositions and prepositional phrases. How did the prepositions help you describe the object?

Write your full response on a separate sheet of paper.

Grammar Activities That Really Grab 'Em!, Grades 3–5 © 2010 by Sarah Glasscock, Scholastic Teaching Resources

Activities: Prepositions

A Stack of Prepositions for a Story

Materials: Two sets of 5 index cards, markers

Give the following directions to pairs: Make a stack of five Preposition cards and a stack of five Noun cards. Write a different preposition on each Preposition card. Write a different noun on each Noun card. Turn each stack of cards facedown. Then exchange the two stacks of cards with another group. With your partner, draw a Preposition card and a Noun card. Work together to make a prepositional phrase and include it in a sentence. This will be the first line of a story. Draw another Preposition card and a Noun card. Make another prepositional phrase. Include it in the next sentence you add to your story.

With the Class: Have pairs share their stories with the rest of the class and talk about how they used prepositional phrases to create their stories. Ask: *Suppose you had made Noun and Pronoun cards. Which pronouns always go with prepositions?*

Every Word You Add

Work with students to write a long sentence. Begin by writing a prepositional phrase on the board or onscreen. Then ask students to take turns doing the following:

- Add another prepositional phrase. Tell your teacher where to write it in the sentence.

- Add a noun or a verb. Tell your teacher where to write it in the sentence.

The sentence has to make sense, so urge students to take time to read it carefully before they add words to it.

With the Class: Discuss the following questions: *How many words long is your sentence? How many prepositions does it have? How many prepositional phrases does it have? How did you decide which words to add? If you added a preposition or a prepositional phrase, how did you decide where to put it in the sentence?*

Draw That Preposition

Tell students to draw a picture that shows a preposition. For example, someone might draw a picture of a girl giving a present to her friend. So that drawing would show the preposition *to*. Before beginning to draw, students should do the following:

- Choose a preposition.
- Think of a sentence that has that preposition in it.
- Draw a picture of that sentence.

Then have them exchange drawings with a partner and guess which preposition their partner is showing.

With the Class: Talk about how students could use the letters of a preposition to show what the preposition means. For example, for the preposition *over*, someone might write the letters *O-V-E-R* in a curve, like a bridge. Below the letters, he or she might draw some wavy lines to show water.

Name _____   Date _____

Prepositions

Jigsaw Puzzle

Some Prepositions

about	above	after	against	at	before
behind	beside	between	beyond	for	in
into	of	off	on	onto	to
toward	under	up	upon	with	without

Write the letter *A* in one of the puzzle pieces. Use prepositions to give clues about where the other pieces are. Tell where each piece in the puzzle is in relation to the *A* piece. Write a clue in each of the other puzzle pieces.

Then cut apart your puzzle. Mix up the pieces. Ask a friend to put the puzzle together. Remind him or her to use the preposition clues.

Example

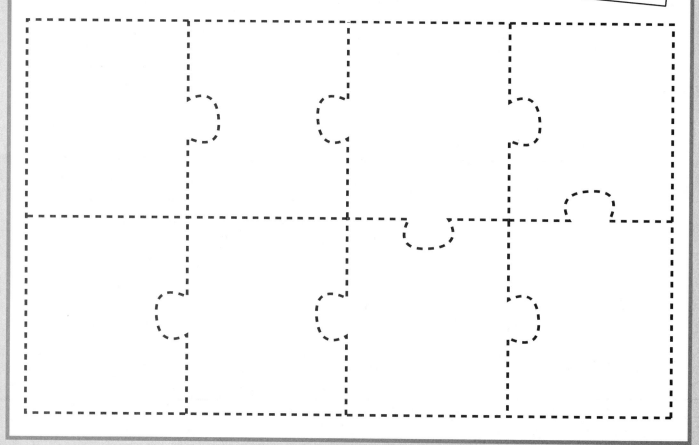

Grammar Activities That Really Grab 'Em!, Grades 3–5 © 2010 by Sarah Glasscock, Scholastic Teaching Resources

All About Singular and Plural Nouns and Verbs

✳ One of the glories of English simplicity is the possibility of using the same word as noun and verb.

—Edward Sapir

A singular noun refers to only one person, animal, thing, or idea, and plural nouns refer to two or more. A singular verb always goes with a singular subject, and a plural verb always goes with a plural subject. This mini-lesson focuses on the following aspects of nouns and verbs:

- **singular and plural nouns**
- **singular and plural verbs**
- **subject-verb agreement**

Introduction

Students trying to make sense of the rules of grammar might not agree with Edward Sapir's opinion about the simplicity of our language. Although the parts of speech are separate compartments, a word such as *fire* can be stored in the noun compartment or in the verb compartment. Then there are the issues of collective nouns and multiple verbs in a sentence, agreement between subjects and verbs, and noun phrases that separate a subject from the verb.

Teach

Distribute copies of the passage "Cinderella Goes Green" on page 37 to students. Read it aloud and ask them to follow along. Then use the teaching guide on page 36 to discuss how the writer used singular and plural nouns and verbs in the passage.

(Also see the lessons on nouns on pages 5–10, verbs on pages 17–22, and subjects and predicates on pages 41–46.)

Apply

Give each student a copy of the Even = Noun, Odd = Verb reproducible on page 40, and go over the list of words. Before pairs begin playing the game, model how you would create a noun sentence and a verb sentence for a word that's not on the list, such as *trick*. Make sure students understand that they are not working with homophones, words that sound the same but are spelled differently.

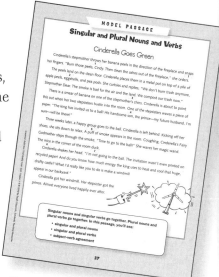

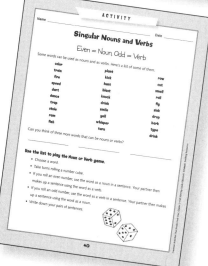

Singular and Plural Nouns

A singular noun names one person, animal, thing, or idea. A plural noun names more than one person, animal, thing, or idea.

KEY POINTS

- A collective noun, such as *team*, describes a group of more than one person, animal, thing, or idea. It can be singular or plural, depending on whether the group is acting as one (singular) or individually (plural): *The group of swallows wheels and turns to the south. The group of birdwatchers drive home in separate cars.* To avoid confusion, suggest that students rewrite sentences that contain collective nouns: *Together, the swallows wheel and turn to the south. The birdwatchers drive home in their separate cars.*

- The British usually use plural verbs with collective nouns, which can sound strange to Americans—*the jury are undecided.*

TEACHING WITH THE MODEL PASSAGE

3 In this sentence, the word *land* is used as a singular noun. *Land* is one of those words that can be used as a noun or a verb.

5 The noun *group* is called a collective noun. Nouns such as *band*, *class*, *team*, and *jury* are collective nouns. They are singular nouns because they refer to a group working together as one.

Singular and Plural Verbs

A singular verb always goes with a singular noun. A plural verb always goes with a plural noun.

KEY POINTS

- Just as a sentence can have more than one subject, it can have more than one verb: *Jack and Jill huff and puff up the hill.* Both verbs must be parallel—have the same tense—and must agree with the single or compound subject.

TEACHING WITH THE MODEL PASSAGE

1 This sentence has two verbs—*throws* and *snaps*. The verbs go with the singular noun, *stepmother*, so both are singular.

2 In this sentence, the word *land* is used as a plural verb.

7 *Duck* is a plural verb. The singular verb is *ducks*. If there had only been one mouse, the sentence would read, *The mouse in the corner of the room ducks.* (*Duck* is another word that can be used as a noun or a verb.)

Subject-Verb Agreement

The subject and verb in a sentence must agree. A singular subject takes a singular verb. A plural subject takes a plural verb.

KEY POINTS

- In a sentence such as *The girl on the swings glides through the air*, students may think that the subject is *swings* because of its location next to the verb *glides*. Emphasize that the subject of the sentence always dictates whether the verb is singular or plural.

- When a collective noun is the subject, a noun phrase often separates it from the verb.

TEACHING WITH THE MODEL PASSAGE

4 In this sentence, the subject is *one* and not *stepsisters*, so the verb has to be singular.

6 The subject of this sentence is *mice*, which is a plural noun—and irregular. The verb is *duck*, which is plural. This subject and verb agree.

Singular and Plural Nouns and Verbs

Cinderella Goes Green

Cinderella's stepmother throws her banana peels in the direction of the fireplace and snaps

her fingers. "Burn those peels, Cindy. Then clean the ashes out of the fireplace," she orders.

The peels land on the clean floor. Cinderella places them in a metal pot on top of a pile of

apple peels, eggshells, and pea pods. She curtsies and replies, "We don't burn trash anymore,

Stepmother Dear. The smoke is bad for the air and the land. We compost our trash now."

There is a smear of banana on one of the stepmother's chins. Cinderella is about to point

this out when her two stepsisters bustle into the room. One of the stepsisters waves a piece of

paper. "The king has invited us to a ball! His handsome son, the prince—my future husband, I'm

sure—will be there!"

Three weeks later, a happy group goes to the ball. Cinderella is left behind. Kicking off her

shoes, she sits down to relax. A puff of smoke appears in the room. Coughing, Cinderella's Fairy

Godmother steps through the smoke. "Time to go to the ball!" She waves her magic wand.

The mice in the corner of the room duck.

Cinderella shakes her head. "I'm not going to the ball. The invitation wasn't even printed on

recycled paper! And do you know how much energy the king uses to heat and cool that huge,

drafty castle? What I'd really like you to do is make a windmill

appear in our backyard."

Cinderella got her windmill. Her stepsister got the

prince. Almost everyone lived happily ever after.

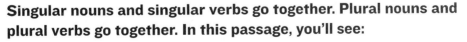

Singular nouns and singular verbs go together. Plural nouns and plural verbs go together. In this passage, you'll see:

- **singular and plural nouns**
- **singular and plural verbs**
- **subject-verb agreement**

Singular and Plural Nouns and Verbs

Teachers: Duplicate these prompts on sturdy paper and then cut them apart. You may also write the prompts on the board or display them onscreen.

Name _____ Date _____

More Characters Move In

Write! A good story has the following elements:

- one or more interesting characters

- a setting that shows where and when the story happens

- a problem

- a description of how the character or characters try to solve the problem

- the solution to the problem

Write a one-paragraph mini-story about one pony, one puppy, or one cow. Then rewrite your story so it's about more than one pony, one puppy, or one cow.

With the Rest of the Class: What did you have to do to change your story from one character to more than one character?

- -

Name _____ Date _____

Follow That Noun Phrase

Write! Complete the sentences with verbs.

The cabin in the woods _____ .

Fourteen pickles in a jar _____ .

The band on the field _____ .

A caterpillar on the leaf _____ and _____ .

With the Rest of the Class: Share your sentences with a small group. Talk about how you decided whether to use a singular or a plural verb to complete each sentence. How were your sentences alike and different?

Activities: Singular and Plural Nouns and Verbs

Book Safari!

> None of the others, not even the goose, noticed that she [Charlotte] was at work.
>
> —from *Charlotte's Web* by E. B. White

 Display this sentence on the board or onscreen so the class can see it. Point out that the subject (*None*) and verb (*noticed*) in the above sentence aren't next to each other. Have students try rewriting the sentence in the present tense. When you've discussed why the agreement is singular (*none—notices*), invite groups on a book safari, giving them these instructions:

- Search through your favorite books for sentences where the subjects and verbs are separated.

- If the sentences are in the past tense, rewrite them in the present tense. (First identify the verb. Then, to find the subject, ask yourself who or what did that action.)

- Record your results in your writing folders or notebooks.

With the Class: Have students share and discuss their results.

A Short Message

Materials: a strip of card stock, colored markers

 Review the characteristics of an effective bumper sticker: the message gives the driver's opinion about something in a short phrase or sentence so people can read it quickly and from a distance. Hand out strips of card stock and have students design a bumper sticker with a two-word message using only one noun and one verb.

With the Class: Display students' bumper stickers on the wall. Ask: *Which ones really jump out at you? Which ones would you put on a car if you owned one? Do you see more singular nouns and verbs or more plural nouns and verbs on the bumper stickers?*

The School Shopping Channel

 Ask students to imagine that your school has its own TV channel called the School Shopping Channel. On it, they can sell items to raise money for your school. Have students work together to write a short script to read on TV. Tell them to think about the following: the product they want to sell, how much it will cost, why they want to sell it, what makes the product special, and what each group member will say. Have them consider how to put together their nouns and verbs. Give them this format for each speaker:

Sam: I'm Sam from Class 4A. Our class needs your help!

With the Class: Set aside time for groups to rehearse their scripts. Then have them perform for the class and take "orders" for their products from the other students. How much money did each group raise?

Name _____ Date _____

Singular Nouns and Verbs

Even = Noun, Odd = Verb

Some words can be used as nouns and as verbs. Here's a list of some of them.

color	plant	row
train	kick	cut
fire	hunt	smell
speed	blast	roll
dart	knock	fly
dance	drink	sink
trap	smile	drop
stole	yell	bark
ram	whisper	type
fish	turn	drink

Can you think of three more words that can be nouns or verbs?

_____   _____   _____

Use the list to play the Noun or Verb game.

- Choose a word.

- Take turns rolling a number cube.

- If you roll an even number, use the word as a noun in a sentence. Your partner then makes up a sentence using the word as a verb.

- If you roll an odd number, use the word as a verb in a sentence. Your partner then makes up a sentence using the word as a noun.

- Write down your pairs of sentences.

Grammar Activities That Really Grab 'Em!, Grades 3–5 © 2010 by Sarah Glasscock, Scholastic Teaching Resources

All About Subjects and Predicates

✳ There is no conversation more boring than the one where everybody agrees.

—Michel De Montaigne

Agreement between two speakers might make their conversation dull, but if the subjects and predicates in their sentences don't agree, then their conversation will be confusing and disagreeable. This mini-lesson focuses on the following aspects of subjects and predicates:

- **subjects**
- **predicates**
- **compound subjects**
- **compound predicates**

Note: Earlier in the book, you'll find the phrase *subject-verb agreement*. This chapter expands the concept of the verb as the predicate (or the key part of the predicate).

Introduction

Begin a mini-lesson on subjects and predicates by writing a short definition for each on the board, for example: "The subject is what or whom the sentence is about. The predicate tells what the subject is or does. The subject and predicate of a sentence must agree. If the subject is singular, the predicate must be singular. If the subject is plural, then the predicate must be plural."

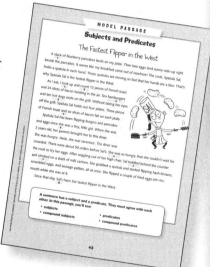

Teach

Distribute copies of the passage "The Fastest Flipper in the West" on page 43 to students. Read it aloud and ask them to follow along. Then use the teaching guide on page 42 to discuss how the writer used subjects and predicates in the passage.

(Also see the lessons on nouns on pages 5–10, verbs on pages 17–22, singular and plural nouns and verbs on pages 35–40, and phrases and clauses on pages 47–52.)

Apply

Duplicate the Agreement Poetry reproducible on page 46 and give a copy to each student. After going over the directions and the example, work with the class to complete the first and second stanzas. Make sure students understand that the noun is the subject and the verb is the predicate. Then have them write the third stanza on their own. Encourage students to compose additional stanzas.

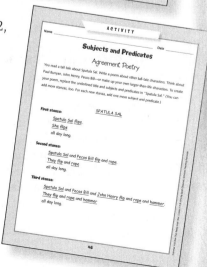

Subjects

The subject tells who or what the sentence is about.

KEY POINTS

- A sentence has a subject and a predicate. They must agree with each other.

- The most important part of the subject is the noun or pronoun (the simple subject).

- A complete subject contains the simple subject and all the words that go with it.

TEACHING WITH THE MODEL PASSAGE

1 The simple subject of this sentence is *stack*, which is singular. The complete subject is *a stack of blueberry pancakes.*

5 *Spatula Sal* is the simple subject of this sentence. The pronoun *she* is part of the clause *since she was a tiny, little girl.* This clause has a subject and a predicate, but it doesn't make sense on its own.

Predicates

The predicate tells what the subject is or does.

KEY POINTS

- The most important part of the predicate is the verb (the simple predicate).

- A complete predicate contains the simple predicate and all the words that go with it.

- Make sure that students understand that the dependent clauses in Points 5 and 6 cannot stand on their own—even though each contains a subject and a verb.

TEACHING WITH THE MODEL PASSAGE

6 This sentence has two pronouns and two verbs, but it only has one subject and one predicate: *She was.* The complete predicate (*was so hungry that she couldn't wait for the cook to fry her eggs*) contains the clause *that she couldn't wait for the cook to fry her eggs*, which can't stand on its own.

8 *Sal's* is a contraction that stands for *Sal has.* This contraction contains the simple subject and part of the simple predicate. The entire simple predicate is *has been.*

Compound Subjects

A compound subject has two or more subjects joined by a coordinating conjunction— and, or, but.

KEY POINTS

- If *and* joins subjects, use a plural predicate: **My sister** *and* **her friends** <u>were screaming</u> during the scary movie.

- If *or* joins the subjects, the subject right before the verb (the simple predicate) determines whether it is singular or plural: **My sister** *or* **her** *friend* <u>was screaming</u> during the scary movie.

TEACHING WITH THE MODEL PASSAGE

3 The compound subjects in this sentence are *hamburgers* and *hot dogs.* Separating the sentences would mean repeating the same words: *Ten hamburgers sizzle on the grill. Ten hot dogs sizzle on the grill.* Good writers try to avoid repetition—unless they want to repeat words for emphasis or rhythmic effect.

4 A compound subject joined by the coordinating conjunction *and* always takes a plural verb.

Compound Predicates

A compound predicate has two or more predicates joined by a coordinating conjunction.

KEY POINTS

- The verbs in the compound predicate must always be the same tense: My sister <u>was screaming</u> during the scary movie, <u>throwing</u> her popcorn into the air, and <u>spilling</u> her bottle of water. Point out that the auxiliary verb, in this case *was*, doesn't have to be repeated with each verb.

TEACHING WITH THE MODEL PASSAGE

2 The main verbs in this sentence are *look* and *count*, and they form a compound predicate. You could rewrite this sentence as two sentences: *As I eat, I look up in the air. I count 12 pieces of French toast and 24 slices of bacon.*

7 Both *toddled* and *climbed* are past-tense verbs.

Subjects and Predicates

The Fastest Flipper in the West

A stack of blueberry pancakes lands on my plate. Then two eggs land sunny-side-up right
beside the pancakes. It seems like my breakfast came out of nowhere! The cook, Spatula Sal,
holds a spatula in each hand. Those spatulas are moving so fast that her hands are a blur. That's
why Spatula Sal is the fastest flipper in the West.

As I eat, I look up and count 12 pieces of French toast
and 24 slices of bacon twisting in the air. Ten hamburgers
and ten hot dogs sizzle on the grill. Without taking her eyes
off the grill, Spatula Sal holds out four plates. Three pieces
of French toast and six slices of bacon fall on each plate.

Spatula Sal has been flipping burgers and pancakes
and eggs since she was a tiny, little girl. When she was
2 years old, her parents brought her to this diner.
She was *hungry*. Heck, she was *ravenous*. The diner was
crowded. There were about 50 orders before Sal's. She was so hungry that she couldn't wait for
the cook to fry her eggs. After wiggling out of her high chair, Sal toddled behind the counter
and climbed on a stack of milk cartons. She grabbed a spatula and started flipping hash browns,
scrambled eggs, and sausage patties, all at once. She flipped a couple of fried eggs into her
mouth while she was at it.

Since that day, Sal's been the fastest flipper in the West.

**A sentence has a subject and a predicate. They must agree with each
other. In this passage, you'll see:**

- **subjects**
- **compound subjects**
- **predicates**
- **compound predicates**

Grammar Activities That Really Grab 'Em! Grades 3–5 © 2010 by Sarah Glasscock, Scholastic Teaching Resources

Subjects and Predicates

Teachers: Duplicate these prompts on sturdy paper and then cut them apart. You may also write the prompts on the board or display them onscreen.

- -

Name _____ Date _____

My Favorite Subject

Write! What are your two favorite subjects in school right now? Math? Social studies? Science? Language arts? Write a short paragraph comparing the two subjects.

With the Rest of the Class: Talk about your favorite subjects. Tell which subjects you used in your paragraphs to talk about your favorite subjects. Did you use only singular subjects? Did you include any compound subjects?

- -

Name _____ Date _____

All Predicate and No Subject?

Write! Read this sentence: *Dance with me!* Does this sentence seem like it's all predicate and no subject? The sentence is an imperative sentence. It gives a command. The subject, *you*, is understood: *[You] dance with me!* Complete the imperative sentences below. Write at least two different sentences for each command.

Go _____ !   Follow _____ !

Take _____ !   Write _____ !

With the Rest of the Class: Share your imperative sentences with a partner. Try to create an imperative sentence that has a compound predicate. Combine one of your commands with one of your partner's.

Grammar Activities That Really Grab 'Em!, Grades 3–5 © 2010 by Sarah Glasscock, Scholastic Teaching Resources

Activities: Subjects and Predicates

That's a Strange Subject

Materials: dictionary

Have students search the dictionary for a noun they aren't familiar with and then write a few sentences about it. Here are some guidelines to give them:

- Use the noun so that anyone would be able to figure out its meaning.

- Make your noun the subject of at least two sentences.

- Underline your noun when you use it as a subject.

Example: The <u>tinnitus</u> [TIN-ih-tus] made Mary clutch her ears. It sounded like an entire hive of bees was buzzing angrily inside her head. "<u>Tinnitus</u> can be caused by many different things," Mary's doctor was saying. Mary couldn't hear him through the buzzing.

With the Class: Tell students to share their sentences with a partner. Have each partner explain whether the underlined subject is singular or plural—and how he or she knows.

The Rules of the Game

Materials: deck of cards, number cubes, and/or spinners

Display a variety of games and their rules for pairs to look at to help them create a new game. It should be a game that at least two people can play. Supply the following guidelines:

- Write down the rules of your game.

- Play the game a few times to make sure it works.

- Rewrite the rules to make them as clear as you can. (Look at the rules for other games.)

- Make sure that all your subjects and predicates agree.

With the Class: Suggest that pairs give their games to other pairs to play and that they keep the following questions in mind: *Were the players able to use the rules to play the game? Can they suggest any changes in the rules to make them clearer?*

A Very Long, Compound Predicate

Say a simple subject, and then call on a student to add a simple predicate to it. As you continue to call on students for simple predicates, write their responses on the board to create one very long sentence. Then work with students to decide which coordinating conjunction or conjunctions—*and, or, but*—to use to connect the simple predicates.

Example: **Teacher:** The cows in the field . . .
Student 1: munched on grass, . . .
Student 2: mooed at the moon, . . .

With the Class: Challenge students to rewrite their very long sentence so it has a subject and only two predicates.

Name _____   Date _____

Subjects and Predicates

Agreement Poetry

You read a tall tale about Spatula Sal. Write a poem about other tall-tale characters. Think about Paul Bunyan, John Henry, Pecos Bill—or make up your own larger-than-life characters. To create your poem, replace the underlined title and subjects and predicates in "Spatula Sal." (You can add more stanzas, too. For each new stanza, add one more subject and predicate.)

SPATULA SAL

First stanza:

Spatula Sal flips.

She flips

all day long.

Second stanza:

Spatula Sal and Pecos Bill flip and rope.

They flip and rope

all day long.

Third stanza:

Spatula Sal and Pecos Bill and John Henry flip and rope and hammer.

They flip and rope and hammer

all day long.

Grammar Activities That Really Grab 'Em!, Grades 3–5 © 2010 by Sarah Glasscock, Scholastic Teaching Resources

All About Phrases and Clauses

✳ If writers stopped writing about what happened to them, then there would be a lot of empty pages.

—Elaine Liner

> The above quote has two phrases and two clauses. A phrase is a group of words without a subject or a predicate: *about what happened* and *of empty pages.* A clause contains a subject and a predicate: *If writers stopped writing,* and *then there would be a lot of empty pages.* This mini-lesson focuses on the following aspects of phrases and clauses:
>
> - **phrases**
> - **independent clauses**
> - **dependent clauses**

Introduction

Begin this mini-lesson by sharing the definitions of phrases and clauses in the box above. As an example, write a related group of phrases and clauses such as the following:

between the front and back wheels (prepositional phrase)

the woman freed the armadillo (independent clause)

when it was trapped (dependent clause)

Ask students how each phrase and clause matches the definitions. Then challenge them to help you combine the phrases and clauses into one sentence. Here's a sample sentence: *The woman freed the armadillo when it was trapped between the front and back wheels.*

Teach

Distribute copies of the passage "Just Like Flying!" on page 49 to students. Read it aloud and ask them to follow along. Then use the teaching guide on page 48 to discuss how the writer used phrases and clauses in the passage.

(Also see the lessons on prepositions on pages 29–34 and sentences on pages 59–64.)

Apply

Duplicate the Add a Phrase Here, a Clause There reproducible on page 52. Give a copy of it and a number cube to each student. Model rolling and recording three numbers and determining whether you can write a sentence. Then allow students to complete the reproducible on their own.

Phrases

A phrase is a group of words that doesn't have a subject and a verb.

KEY POINTS

- A prepositional phrase begins with a preposition and ends with a noun or an object pronoun: *with Jacqui, with me, with Jacqui and me.*

- A sentence can have more than one prepositional phrase.

- A participial phrase begins with a present or past participle: <u>*Enjoying the cool weather,*</u> *the queen walked three miles. The court jester,* <u>*tired from the long walk,*</u> *staggered behind her.* Emphasize that these phrases do not have subjects.

TEACHING WITH THE MODEL PASSAGE

2 This sentence has the phrase *impressed by roller coasters*. The phrase has a past-tense verb (*impress + –ed*) in it called a past participle. A comma sets it off because it comes at the beginning of a sentence.

3 This sentence has the phrase *tumbling onto the ground*. The phrase has a present-tense verb (*tumble + –ing*) in it called a present participle.

4 This sentence has two prepositional phrases: *in love* and *with flying*.

7 Always use an object pronoun—*me, you, it, him, his, her, us, you, them*—in a prepositional phrase.

Independent Clauses

An independent clause has a subject and a predicate. It can stand alone as a sentence.

KEY POINTS

- Two or more independent clauses can be joined together with a coordinating conjunction—*for, and, nor, but, or, yet, so.* (Remember the word FANBOYS.)

TEACHING WITH THE MODEL PASSAGE

5 The coordinating conjunction *but* joins these two independent clauses.

8 This clause has a subject—*thousands*—and a predicate—*fly*. It forms a complete sentence on its own, so it's an independent clause.

Dependent Clauses

A dependent clause has a subject and a predicate, but it can't stand alone as a sentence.

KEY POINTS

- A dependent clause begins with a relative pronoun—*who, that, which, what*—or a subordinating conjunction—*if, when, before, since.*

- When a dependent clause goes before an independent clause, it is set off by a comma.

TEACHING WITH THE MODEL PASSAGE

1 *When 10-year-old Amelia Earhart saw her first airplane* is a dependent clause. It is combined with an independent clause and set off with a comma to make a complete sentence. Since the dependent clause starts the sentence, it's set off by a comma.

6 The dependent clause in this sentence is *as the red plane zoomed past her*. Since it appears at the end of the sentence, it's not set off by a comma.

Phrases and Clauses

Just Like Flying!

When 10-year-old Amelia Earhart saw her first airplane, she wasn't very excited. She
1
described the plane as "a thing of rusty wire and wood and not at all interesting."

More impressed by roller coasters, Amelia tried to build one in her backyard. The ramp
2
started at the top of a toolshed and ended on the ground. Amelia climbed into a box and slid
down the ramp, tumbling onto the ground at the bottom. Despite a hurt lip and a torn dress,
3
Amelia had a huge smile on her face. She described her ride as "just like flying!"

About ten years later, Amelia finally fell in love with flying. She was at an air show where
4
pilots were doing stunts and tricks. One pilot spotted Amelia and a friend standing in an open
area. He dove and aimed his plane at them. The friend ran for cover, but Amelia didn't move.
5
She thought she might like to be flying as the red plane zoomed past her.
6

Then, when Amelia finally flew in a plane, she wanted to be pilot, too. Soon she became the
first woman to fly by herself across North America and back again. During her short life, Amelia
continued to make many other record-breaking flights.

Today, a plane ride probably doesn't seem like such a big deal to you and me. Thousands of
7   **7**   **8**
people fly every day. Still, the next time you fly, or you look up in the sky and see a plane, think
8
about Amelia Earhart.

> **A phrase is a group of words. A clause is a group of words that
> contains a subject and a predicate. In this passage, you'll see:**
>
> - **phrases**
> - **independent and dependent clauses**

Grammar Activities That Really Grab 'Em!, Grades 3–5 © 2010 by Sarah Glasscock, Scholastic Teaching Resources

Phrases and Clauses

Teachers: Duplicate these prompts on sturdy paper and then cut them apart. You may also write the prompts on the board or display them onscreen.

Name _____ Date _____

I'm Going Through a Phrase

Write! Choose one of the following prepositional or participial phrases. Include it in the lead of a scary short story.

- in the darkness at the bottom of the stairs
- barking at the black shape
- dashing for the safety of my room
- buried in the backyard

With the Rest of the Class: Talk about these questions: How did you use the phrase to set a scary mood for your story? What other phrases do you see in your story?

Name _____ Date _____

The Clause of It All

Write! Choose one of the following clauses. Include it in a sentence. Make that sentence the lead of a funny short story.

- that made the stack of cereal boxes tumble down
- since my dog ate my homework
- the ketchup spurted out of the bottle
- who accidentally put on one blue sock and one red sock

With the Rest of the Class: Talk about these questions: How did you use the clause to write a sentence? How did you use that lead to set a funny mood for your story? What other clauses do you see in your story?

Grammar Activities That Really Grab 'Em!, Grades 3–5 © 2010 by Sarah Glasscock, Scholastic Teaching Resources

ACTIVITIES: Phrases and Clauses

A Hide-and-Seek Story Using Prepositional Phrase Clues

Materials: drawing materials including paper, colored pencils, and markers

SMALL GROUP Have students work together to write and illustrate a picture book about characters playing hide and seek. The group should use prepositional phrases to show where the characters hide and where they look for each other. For each page of text, they should draw a picture that shows the action and write a caption for each picture. The caption should be in the form of a prepositional phrase. For example, if the drawing shows a boy hiding underneath the bed, the caption might read "underneath the bed."

With the Class: Have two groups meet and talk about how they used prepositional phrases in their stories. Ask them to read each other's stories and offer positive comments.

The Clause Convention

Materials: index cards, markers, safety pins

WHOLE CLASS Form two teams—the Dependent Clauses and the Independent Clauses. Then count off students. Even numbers will write the appropriate clause about the topic of pickles. Odd numbers will write the appropriate clause about the topic of onions. You may also choose your own related topics. Share why people hold conventions (to share information and ideas about common topics) and have students participate in a class Clause Convention with these instructions:

- Create your own name tags. Be sure to include your name and whether you're a Dependent or an Independent Clause.

- Wear your name tag and look for someone at the convention who has the same interest as yours—pickles or onions. See if you can combine your clauses to create a sentence that makes sense.

With the Class: When students can form a clear sentence, write it on the board. Send students back to the convention to see who else they can make a sentence with.

"If Only" Clause Poems

 Direct pairs to write an "If only" poem. The first line is a dependent "if only" clause. **PAIR** The second line is an independent "then" clause that tells what would happen if their wish came true. The third and fourth lines of the stanza repeat the pattern:

If only . . . ,
Then . . . .
If only . . . ,
Then . . . .
Challenge pairs to try to write at least three stanzas.

With the Class: Tell pairs to practice reading aloud their poem—one partner will read lines 1 and 3 in each stanza, and the other partner will read lines 2 and 4—and then perform it for the class. Talk about the similarities and differences among the poems.

Name _____ Date _____

Phrases and Clauses

Add a Phrase Here, a Clause There

Materials: Number cube

In this activity, each number you roll stands for a type of phrase or clause. See the key below.

> **1** = Independent Clause that begins with a proper noun
>
> **2** = Dependent Clause that begins with "when"
>
> **3** = Phrase that begins with "down"
>
> **4** = Present Participial Phrase that begins with "going"
>
> **5** = Past Participial Phrase that begins with "hooted"

Roll the number cube three times. Write the number you rolled and the phrase or clause you create in the chart.

Number Rolled	**Phrase or Clause**
_____	_____
_____	_____
_____	_____

Can you create a complete sentence from your phrases and/or clauses? If you can, write it below. If you can't, keep rolling numbers until you can. Write down your numbers, and phrases and clauses. Then write your sentence below.

_____

_____

_____

_____

All About Elaboration

✳ Once you've got some words looking back at you, you can take two
or three—or throw them away and look for others.

—Bernard Malamud

> In writing, elaboration is the act or process of making our work clearer
> and richer. As described in the above quote, elaboration involves
> adding, deleting, and replacing words. This mini-lesson focuses on the
> following aspects of elaboration:
>
> - **adding details to make writing more specific**
> - **adding details to make writing more descriptive**
> - **taking out details**

Introduction

Begin the mini-lesson on elaboration by writing the Bernard Malamud
quote on the board. Ask students what they think Malamud's words
mean. Explain that Malamud is talking about elaboration—adding
words, deleting words, or replacing words to make a piece of writing
stronger and clearer. Then write the following sentence on the
board: *The dog barked.* Ask students for suggestions on how to make
the sentence more specific and descriptive.

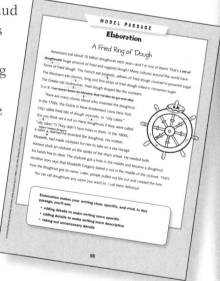

Teach

Distribute copies of the passage "A Fried Ring of Dough" on page
55 to students. Read it aloud and ask them to follow along. Then
use the teaching guide on page 54 to discuss how the writer used
elaboration in the passage.

   (Also see the lessons on nouns on pages 5–10, verbs on
pages 17–22, and adjectives and adverbs on pages 23–28.)

Apply

Duplicate the How Blue Am I? reproducible on page 58 and
give a copy to each student. After going over the directions,
model how you would choose something in the classroom
that is blue and create a paint color name to describe that
shade of blue. It could be a wall color, a piece of clothing,
the cover of a book, or a student's eye color. When students
have completed the reproducible, place them in groups so
they can share and compare their paint colors.

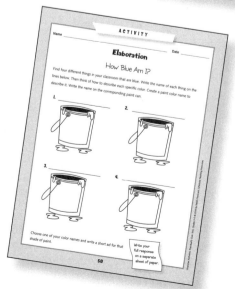

Adding Details to Make Writing More Specific

Be specific about names, places, and other information.

KEY POINTS

- Ernest Hemingway once said, "All our words from loose using have lost their edge." Words like *very*, *a lot*, and *really* don't add specific details to our writing. We need to use words that still have their edge.

TEACHING WITH THE MODEL PASSAGE

2 The writer gives three specific examples of countries and their fried-dough treats.

6 The writer adds the name of the sailor. If you had invented something, wouldn't you want everyone to know your name?

Adding Details to Make Writing More Descriptive

Use details to create vivid pictures in readers' minds.

KEY POINTS

- Even nonfiction—especially nonfiction—needs descriptive details.

- Encourage students to incorporate sensory images into their writing. The sentence *The dog is big and nice* doesn't give a reader many clues, but the sentence *That black Lab is as tall as a Shetland pony, but he's as gentle as a lamb* helps readers clearly picture the dog.

TEACHING WITH THE MODEL PASSAGE

1 Compare the two phrases *a lot of doughnuts* and *a huge amount of fried and sugared dough*. What picture pops into your mind when you read each phrase?

4 Again, the writer gives the specific name of the Dutch treat *olykoeks*, and that it means "oily cakes" in English.

Taking Out Details

Stay on topic. When you read your writing, look for details that don't belong or that you've repeated.

KEY POINTS

- Every word has to count. In our eagerness to convey *exactly* what we mean in our writing, it can be easy to include too many details that are repetitive or are unnecessary.

- We sometimes fall in love with some of the words we use and hate to give them up. If we don't take out repetitive or unnecessary details, we may lose our audience.

TEACHING WITH THE MODEL PASSAGE

3 The writer loses sight of the topic. She may want to go to Mexico but that doesn't have anything to do with doughnuts, so she deleted the last sentence.

5 Some readers might feel that this is unnecessary information. However, the writer has placed this sentence in parentheses to show she knows it isn't completely necessary. It could be cut, but the writer steps in at the beginning and end of the passage, so she is being true to her voice in this passage.

Elaboration

A Fried Ring of Dough

Americans eat about 10 billion doughnuts each year—and I'm one of them! That's a ~~lot of~~
~~doughnuts!~~ huge amount of fried and sugared dough! Many cultures around the world have
1
forms of fried dough. The French eat *beignets*, pillows of fried dough covered in powered sugar.
2
The Mexicans eat *churros*, long and thin strips of fried dough rolled in cinnamon sugar.
2
The Greeks eat *loukoumas*, fried dough shaped like the numbers
2
0 or 8. ~~I've never been to Mexico, but I'd like to go one day.~~
3

There are many stories about who invented the doughnut.
In the 1700s, the Dutch in New Amsterdam (now New York
City) called fried bits of dough *olykoeks*, or "oily cakes."
4
(Do you think we'd eat so many doughnuts if they were called
5
"oily cakes"?) They didn't have holes in them. In the 1800s,
named Hanson Gregory
a sailor ∧ claimed he invented the doughnut. His mother,
6
Elizabeth, had made *olykoeks* for him to take on a sea voyage.
Hanson stuck an *olykoek* on the spoke of the ship's wheel. He needed both
his hands free to steer. The *olykoek* got a hole in the middle and became a doughnut.
Another story says that Elizabeth Gregory baked a nut in the middle of the *olykoek*. That's
how the doughnut got its name. Later, people pulled out the nut and created the hole.

You can call doughnuts any name you want to. I call them delicious!

**Elaboration makes your writing clear, specific, and vivid. In this
passage, you'll see:**

- **adding details to make writing more specific**
- **adding details to make writing more descriptive**
- **taking out unnecessary details**

Elaboration

Teachers: Duplicate these prompts on sturdy paper and then cut them apart. You may also write the prompts on the board or display them onscreen.

Name _____ Date _____

Would You Elaborate on That?

Write! Think about a penny. Quickly write down as many words and phrases that come to your mind about the coin. Use them in the box below. Then write a paragraph describing a penny. Choose which words from the box to include.

> Write your full response on a separate sheet of paper.

> **A penny . . .**

With the Rest of the Class: Share words and phrases from the box so your teacher can list them on the board. Which words did you use, too? Which words most surprised you?

Name _____ Date _____

One More Detail

Write! Create a character to write a story about. Begin by writing whether it's a person or an animal—or something else. Then add details, one line at a time. Get more and more specific with your details. Aim for at least ten lines of description.

Example

- character
- simple description
- increasingly detailed description

With the Rest of the Class: Share your list with the rest of the class. Talk about how you created your character. How did you decide which details to add? Were you able to see your character more clearly the more details you added?

> Write your full response on a separate sheet of paper.

Grammar Activities That Really Grab 'Em!, Grades 3–5 © 2010 by Sarah Glasscock, Scholastic Teaching Resources

ACTIVITIES: Elaboration

Combine-and-Refine Shared Writing

Select a variety of objects for groups to study, such as a holiday ornament, a fabric swatch, a pickle, a maraca or other musical instrument, and so on. Give an object to each group. Allow time for everyone in a group to study the object. Then ask each member to write a description of the object. Urge students to make their descriptions as clear and rich as they can and to use their senses to help them describe the object. After everyone shares their writing, have group members work together to combine all their descriptions and refine them into one description.

With the Class: After a student from each group reads aloud its final description to the rest of the class, ask the other groups: *Can you guess what their object is?*

Could You Be More Specific?

When you describe how to do something, you have to be very specific. Each step has to be written down clearly and in order. Give the following instructions for writing how-to's in pairs:

- Think about something you both know how to do or something you both know how to make. *Do not talk to each other about the steps or any other details.*

- After one of you writes the first step, the other one writes the next step. Trade off until your how-to is complete.

- Now you can read the entire how-to together and talk about the steps.

- Decide together whether the how-to is specific enough. Add, replace, or take away details to make your how-to clear and specific.

With the Class: Have pairs exchange how-tos. Can they make any suggestions so the other pair's how-to is more specific? Do they think they could successfully follow the steps in the how-to?

News Flash! Take It Away!

Material: newspapers

Newspapers use headlines to tell what a story is about. A really good headline is short, but it has to have enough information to grab a reader's attention.

Americans Gobbled Up 10 Billion Doughnuts Last Year

With students, study the headlines in the newspapers. Then challenge them to think about what they did yesterday. What were the highlights of their day? Challenge students to write headlines that describe their day. Remind them to keep the headlines short and to take out any information they really don't need.

With the Class: Have students share headlines with a partner and ask pairs to think about these questions: *Which headlines really caught your partner's attention? Which headlines did he or she think could be cut even more?*

Name _____   Date _____

Elaboration

How Blue Am I?

Find four different things in your classroom that are blue. Write the name of each thing on the lines below. Then think of how to describe each specific color. Create a paint color name to describe it. Write the name on the corresponding paint can.

1. _____

2. _____

3. _____

4. _____

Choose one of your color names and write a short ad for that shade of paint.

Write your full response on a separate sheet of paper.

Grammar Activities That Really Grab 'Em!, Grades 3–5 © 2010 by Sarah Glasscock, Scholastic Teaching Resources

All About Sentences

✱ One day the Nouns were clustered in the street.
An Adjective walked by, with her dark beauty.
The Nouns were struck, moved, changed.
The next day a Verb drove up, and created the Sentence.

—Kenneth Koch

A sentence can consist of just one word—"Go!"—or it can contain complex combinations of every part of speech. This mini-lesson focuses on the following aspects of sentences:

- **types of sentences**
- **simple sentences**
- **combining sentences**
- **complex sentences**

Introduction

Begin the mini-lesson on sentences by writing on the board a short definition such as the following: "A sentence is a group of words that expresses a complete thought. It must always contain a subject and a verb: After he left school, <u>Lester ran</u> home and <u>changed</u> into his baseball uniform." Then discuss Kenneth Koch's explanation of a sentence at the top of the page. Ask students to use what they've learned about the parts of speech to explain Koch's words.

Teach

Distribute copies of the passage "A Fish That's a Poor Swimmer?" on page 61 to students. Read it aloud and ask them to follow along. Then use the teaching guide on page 60 to discuss the variety of sentences in the passage.

(Also see the lessons on phrases and clauses on pages 47–52 and the other lessons as necessary.)

Apply

Duplicate the Spin a Sentence reproducible on page 64 and give a copy to each student. Review the examples of the simple, compound, and complex sentences at the top of the page. Then go over the directions with students and make sure they understand how to use a pencil and a paper clip to make the spinner operational. Model spinning and writing the corresponding kind of sentence. Point out to students that they can write any type of sentence—declarative, interrogative, exclamatory, or imperative.

Types of Sentences

There are four types of sentences: declarative, interrogative, exclamatory, and imperative.

KEY POINTS

- Declarative sentences are statements.

- Interrogative sentences are questions.

- Exclamatory sentences show strong feeling and end with exclamation points.

- Imperative sentences give commands.

- A sentence can be a combination of types, for example, both exclamatory and imperative. Talk about whether other combinations are possible, such as a sentence that is both interrogative and imperative or both declarative and exclamatory.

TEACHING WITH THE MODEL PASSAGE

1 The first sentence in this passage is a question, so it's an interrogative sentence.

8 The last sentence in this passage is a command—and it shows strong feeling—so it's both an imperative and an exclamatory sentence.

Simple Sentences

A simple sentence is an independent clause.

KEY POINTS

- A simple sentence has one subject and one verb—although the subject and/or verb might be compound.

TEACHING WITH THE MODEL PASSAGE

3 This simple sentence is probably the shortest sentence in the passage. It explains what kind of fish sea horses are.

6 Although this sentence contains a prepositional phrase, it's still a simple sentence.

Compound Sentences

A compound sentence is composed of two or more complete sentences (independent clauses).

KEY POINTS

- Coordinating conjunctions—*for, and, nor, but, or, yet, so*—or semicolons can be used to combine the sentences. Except in very short sentences, a comma goes before the coordinating conjunction.

- Talk about how combining sentences with the conjunction *but* affects their relationship. If the sentences had remained separate, some kind of qualifier would be needed, such as *however* or *though*.

TEACHING WITH THE MODEL PASSAGE

2 The coordinating conjunction *and* combines these two sentences: *This tiny fish has a head shaped like a horse's. Its tail is long and curved and can grasp things like a monkey's.*

7 The coordinating conjunction *but* combines these two sentences: *Sea horses may be poor swimmers. Their home really is the sea.*

Complex Sentences

A complex sentence consists of an independent clause and one or more dependent clauses.

KEY POINTS

- When a dependent clause begins the sentence, it is set off with a comma.

- Show students that the dependent clauses in the complex sentences in the passage can be moved to another position within the sentence without changing its meaning.

TEACHING WITH THE MODEL PASSAGE

4 The dependent clause that begins this complex sentence is *Instead of scales* and is set off with a comma.

5 The dependent clause in this complex sentence is *because they blend into the background.*

Sentences

A Fish That's a Poor Swimmer?

What do you get if you cross a horse, a monkey, a kangaroo, and
a chameleon? You get a sea horse! This tiny fish has a head shaped like
a horse's, and its tail is long and curved and can grasp things like
a monkey's. The male sea horse carries eggs in a pouch until the babies
are born. Finally, the eyes of a sea horse can move independently
like a chameleon's. Sea horses really do look like some kind of
prehistoric creature.

They are bony fish. Instead of scales, their thin skin covers a chain of bony rings.
Sea horses suck food out of the water through their long snouts. They'll eat anything
that will go through their snouts.

Sea horses are poor swimmers, so they spend most of their time hanging out in
sea grass. Holding on to the blades of grass with their tails, they escape being eaten by other
larger fish. Sea horses can also change color. This helps them avoid being eaten, too, because
they blend into the background.

Did you notice I said that the males and not the females carry the eggs? The female deposits
her eggs in the male's pouch. Then he fertilizes the eggs and carries them for about two weeks
to a month until the babies are born. Like other fish, babies are called "fry." A male sea horse
can produce anywhere from 5 to 200 fry.

Sea horses may be poor swimmers, but their home really is the sea. Don't try to raise one in
your aquarium at home!

**A sentence has a subject and a verb. It expresses a complete thought.
In this passage, you'll see:**

- **different types of sentences**
- **compound sentences**
- **simple sentences**
- **complex sentences**

Grammar Activities That Really Grab 'Em!, Grades 3–5 © 2010 by Sarah Glasscock, Scholastic Teaching Resources

Sentences

Name _____ Date _____

I Like Your Type

Write! Imagine this scene: A kid is carrying a skateboard up a hill in a park and accidentally drops it. Write a four-sentence short story about what happens to the runaway skateboard. Include each type of sentence, in any order, in your story: declarative, interrogative, exclamatory, and imperative.

> Write your full response on a separate sheet of paper.

With the Rest of the Class: Share your story with the rest of the class. Talk about the similarities and differences among your stories.

Name _____ Date _____

My Life So Far

Write! Suppose you wrote a book about your life up to this point. What would the first paragraph of your book be? Would you start at the very beginning? Would you start with today? Would you start with the most exciting thing that has ever happened to you? Would you start with the very first memory you have? Would you start with a family story about you as baby?

After jotting down your ideas, write that first paragraph. Read your draft. Think about the sentences. Do they all begin the same way: subject then verb? Revise your paragraph to include a variety of simple, compound, and complex sentences.

With the Rest of the Class: Your teacher may collect your paragraphs in a folder or notebook with the title *Our Lives So Far: Chapter One*. Read everyone's paragraph. What do you notice about the variety of sentences you see? Write your comments on a sticky note and attach it to each paragraph. Be sure to sign your note.

To the Teacher: Collect students' paragraphs in a folder or notebook and supply sticky notes to students.

Grammar Activities That Really Grab 'Em!, Grades 3–5 © 2010 by Sarah Glasscock, Scholastic Teaching Resources

ACTIVITIES: Sentences

That's Simple

Have pairs work together to create a choral poem. For each stanza of the poem, they should complete the simple sentences below by recognizing whether they need to supply a singular or a plural noun and verb.

There's a (noun) behind the (noun).

A (noun) (verb) behind the (noun).

There are (noun) behind the (noun).

(noun) (verb) behind the (noun).

Pairs should take turns reading aloud the lines of the choral poem.

Example of a stanza:

Partner 1: There's a <u>pig</u> behind the <u>couch</u>.   *Partner 2:* A <u>pig</u> <u>slides</u> behind the <u>couch</u>.

Partner 1: There are <u>giraffes</u> behind the <u>door</u>.   *Partner 2:* <u>Giraffes</u> <u>hide</u> behind the <u>door</u>.

With the Class: Set aside time for pairs to perform their choral poems for the class and then answer any questions the audience has.

Compound Interest

Have each group review a favorite picture book. Each member reads it independently and then writes his or her opinion of it in two or three sentences. Then tell students to work together to decide how to combine some of their individual sentences to create a group review of the book. Remind them to use coordinating conjunctions to combine the sentences: *for, and, nor, but, or, yet, so.*

With the Class: Have groups present their opinions orally or in written form. If they choose an oral presentation, allow time for them to practice, and then share it with the class. Ask groups to talk about how they worked together to combine the sentences.

Growing Sentences, Word by Word

Materials: Ten index cards, a marker for each student

Play a sentence game with the group. Have each student write down a different word on each of ten index cards, including a variety of nouns, verbs, adjectives, adverbs, and prepositions. Give students these directions to play:

• Combine all your cards, shuffle them, and turn them facedown on a table or a desk.

• Take turns drawing a card. When everyone has a card, try to put them together to form a sentence. If you can't form a sentence, take turns drawing a new card until you can. Write it down. Then decide whether you can rearrange the words to rewrite the sentence.

• See how many sentences you can form before you run out of cards.

With the Class: Merge two groups. Have them try to combine a sentence from each group using coordinating conjunctions—*for, and, nor, but, or, yet, so.* Ask students to identify the type of sentences they created—declarative, interrogative, exclamatory, or imperative.

Name _____ **Date** _____

SENTENCES

Spin a Sentence

A sentence can be simple, compound, or complex.

Simple sentence: The dish ran away with the spoon.

Compound sentence: The dish ran away with the spoon, but the knife and fork stayed home.

Complex sentence: When the dish ran away with the spoon, the knife and fork felt very lonely.

Let the spinner tell you what kind of sentence to write. (The picture above shows how to use a pencil and a paper clip to create the spinner.) Spin the spinner six times. Write your sentences on a separate sheet of paper.

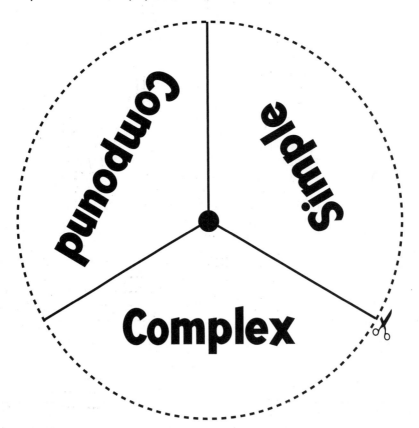

Grammar Activities That Really Grab 'Em!, Grades 3–5 © 2010 by Sarah Glasscock, Scholastic Teaching Resources